What others are saying about this book:

*"Tom Hale really **tells it like it is!** He provides great information on how to be successful in the real estate business whether you are a seasoned veteran or a new person in the business. I wish I could have read Tom's book 32 years ago when I was new in the real estate business!"*

-Craig Cooley
   Top producing real estate broker.
   Prudential NW Properties

"The New Age Real Estate Agent gives the confidence and motivation new brokers need to succeed. It is the one and only guide you need to be successful in the real estate industry and in life!"

-Yulee Chang
   Real Estate Broker

"Tom Hale removes the shroud over what it takes to be a successful Realtor & live a life with balance. Tom has been a mentor to me for the last 7 years and has impacted my personal & business life in ways that have drastically improved them. Tom can take the guesswork out of this business for any agent & help turn their business & life around, I've witnessed this personally."

- Norman Sinai
Top 100 agents, Coldwell Banker
Pleasanton, California

"If you are looking for a magic pill this isn't it, and if you are looking to be successful at the business of selling real estate, then all you need to do is follow Tom's simple instructions."

-Nathan Jones
Top Producing Broker
Prudential NW Properties

The New Age Real Estate Agent

"Thomas R Hale is a true Leader. Are you looking for a balance between home and business? Then this book will give you the insight that you need to have balance in your life and live life to the fullest without any limitations. Not only has he earned his success with integrity but he has enjoyed doing it. He is not only my husband, business partner, and friend. He is also a Teacher who has taught me that Sales is the best career to be in. That the only limitations in life are the ones you give yourself. This book will help you mold your own key to happiness and wealth mastery."

-Lizbeth Hale
CEO of Lendingman Mortgage Services PC
The Hale Group, Inc. Real Estate

"I have been a Real Estate Agent for 9 years. Since reading this book, I find myself more focused on my goals, more excited about my business and much more confident. For the first time in my career I know exactly what to do (because of the system) in order to achieve my goals. The fact that Tom actually works this system instead of merely talking about it makes it easier to follow. Now it's up to me...Thanks Tom!"

-Kedric Wells
Re/Max Equity Group

The New Age Real Estate Agent
A simple process to make millions!

By Thomas Hale

Revised Edition
2008

Lito Publishing · Clackamas, Oregon

The New Age Real Estate Agent

The New Age Real Estate Agent

The New Age Real Estate Agent
A simple process to make millions!

By Thomas Hale

Published by:
Lito Publishing
14674 SE Sunnyside Rd #219
Clackamas, OR 97015

Unattributed quotations are by Thomas Hale

ISBN print edition	9780978935948
ISBN PDF edition	0-9789359-1-8
ISBN eBook edition	0-9789359-2-6
ISBN CD recorded edition	0-9789359-3-4

Contents

The New Age Real Estate Agent

The New Age Real Estate Agent

The New Age Real Estate Agent

To my beautiful wife, Lizbeth who is a wonderful mom and my best friend.

I will never forget the time you played a prank on me in Maui with the car radio, making me believe for the whole trip that the radio was voice activated. While you sat in the backseat with our baby changing the radio stations on the secondary controls and fooling me the whole time!
Don't let your guard down...

payback will soon come.

The New Age Real Estate Agent

Introduction

As my wife and I sit here in our beautiful home with all the amenities and a tremendous view, we look back on all the hard work that it took us to have such a wonderful life. Nice cars, grand pianos and most of the material things that we have always wanted are ours for the taking now – not to mention, the new level of spirituality we have arrived at, too.

It has not always been this way, but through hard work in real estate and investing in ourselves to become better people, we are making our dreams come true daily.

So, it is with this book that I would like to convey an important message to you. That message is how to become a better person that focuses on the key areas in your life that are most important to you.

If you are all about the following, then this book is for you:

-Giving and making a change in life and business;
-Learning the systems in this book and applying them without doubt;
-Having some fun and variety in your life and not getting bored like most agents;
- Having mass recognition from others, like being a role model or a recognized leader in your community or industry;
 -Growing to your highest potential as a business owner and human being.
I was fortunate enough to learn at a very young age the

power of my mind and how I and others can make things happen. I never really quite understood it, but I just knew it was there all along.

Now, through these pages you will learn how to have a happy, well-balanced life by applying some real and simple techniques. The techniques that I talk about are very real and easy to develop and learn. Many of the stories you will be able to relate to and apply to your life and business with ease.

Selling real estate should be an easy process that you should enjoy doing, not dreading. By developing a great cookie cutter system, you will learn how to do numerous deals with minimum effort and maximum results!

I also give a lot of credit to my wife for being so patient and understanding in our daily lives and for this is how we grow together. It has not always been easy, nothing worth it in life ever is but we have always tried to base our lives coming from a foundation of love and contribution. By knowing this and practicing it daily has made the biggest change in our lives ever.

The New Age Real Estate Agent

The New Age Real Estate Agent

Chapter 1

Whether New Or A Veteran To Real Estate, You Can Start Now The Right Way!

"The reason most people face the future with apprehension instead of anticipation is because they don't have it well designed."
Jim Rohn

Of all the professions in the world that one can get into and make a grand living at, real estate and sales are among the most rewarding and highest paid. However, like in any field one enters, if you want a highly successful and rewarding life, you have to pay your dues.

Most people get into real estate because they see the freedom of being their own boss and the glamour of making a lot of money. Little do they know that when they first receive their real estate license, the clock begins ticking. Time is not on their side. There is a 75% chance that after a person receives their real estate license, they will turn it back in as inactive status within 18 months.

Why is this? Why does someone first start out with a dream to be their own boss, a dream to make a lot of money and all the freedom that comes with it, to quit after only 1 ½ years on average? The reason is quite simple – they take the same old ways of learning something new and apply it to their new profession and think that this time it will be different. What I have found over the years is that if only they just applied a few new habits in their life, they would have succeeded and flourished in the new field.

When I first received my real estate license, I sat at a desk and was told that I had floor time that day by my broker. "What is floor time?" I asked. I thought to myself, "I thought I was going to be my own boss now."

The broker astonishingly turned with a smile on his face, looked me in the eye, and asked, "Nobody ever told you about floor time?"

"Well...no," I replied.

After he explained it all to me, I thought the money was going to come even easier than I first imagined. People will be flocking through the front door with bags of money or bills gushing out of their pockets!

"This is the easiest, most rewarding job I have ever had!" I thought.

What a small mind I had. The money never came in truckloads; it didn't even come in Tonka truckloads. It simply never came! "This isn't why I got into real estate! I want to make some good money. I want to be my own boss," I thought to myself.

Most people get their licenses and start working right away for a broker that they found by interviewing them, because this is the norm and this is what everyone tells them to do. What do they look for when deciding what broker or company to work for? Most brokers are just looking for warm bodies to fill offices and will hire an inexperienced agent on the spot. Why? Because they have to pay the rent, that's why!

The power brokers of today are smarter than that and want to be profitable. These brokers will focus on having more top producers and more unity in the office, all by doing the same thing – and that is being coached by someone that has been through the trenches. These smart brokers hire someone to help them out so they can be more profitable and run a successful business.

Beware of the brokers that want to just fill up the office with warm bodies; they realize that it is a numbers game. They know that the more agents that they have working for them, the more money and security they will have. Why? Because the average agent in North America sells only about three to five homes a year! So if you think about it, if a broker has 60 agents and most of them are on a split commission at 50/50 or 60/40 (in which broker gets 40% of everything the agents bring in), then you have one happy broker. Of course, there will be a few top agents in his company and he will use these top producers as a way to get more agents to work for him – meaning that he or she will brag to a new trainee that their office does $100 million a year or so.

 Unknowingly to the new trainee, 95% of that business comes from the top producers in the company.

The New Age Real Estate Agent

Therefore, the smart brokers of today are turning their offices around and focusing on top producers or training their agents to be highly skilled and knowledgeable. They want an office filled with them, not just a few of them.

Choosing Your Broker

So therefore, when deciding on a broker to work for, find one that is behind your success and is willing to help you grow as a business professional. You can also find out about their family life too. Do they spend all their time in the office and have no family and no life? Do they own other businesses? Is it someone that can help you truly become who you were intended to be?

Look at what area you want to work in. If you live in a major metropolitan area, you have low-priced and high-priced homes. Take my advice and go work the high-priced areas, even if you don't live there. Interview several brokers in that area and don't just pick a well-known national or international company just because you think you will do better there. It's not about the company and how well they do in that area, it's all about <u>you</u> and how hard <u>you</u> work. Let me say that again, it's not about the company you work for; it's how hard <u>you</u> work! If you hardly work, then you hardly get paid. Work hard everyday and the universe will happily pay you. But you also need the backing of a great broker or a great coach – someone that has done not just great, but exceptional in the field. For example, if you wanted to be the best in the world at boxing, don't you agree that it would be smart to learn from or model yourself after the great Mohamed Ali or any other world-class boxers alive today? Or if you wanted to become a U.S. senator, wouldn't it make sense to model after the best out there? So if you wanted to become a great real estate agent, doctor, lawyer or whatever, wouldn't it make sense to model and learn from the best? You are in luck then, my friend, for you have a very powerful book in your hands that will outline for you just how to do so.

So first, ask yourself what is the best? Does it mean:
-Best in customer service?
-Best in most transactions?
-Best in most money made per year?
-Best in what?

Hiring a trainer

If you are a new agent – or even if you are not new and would like to simply take your business to the next level – you should highly consider hiring a real estate trainer or coach, someone that is considered the best in the business. The use of mentors and trainers is growing at a very fast rate, and I am huge supporter of mentors and trainers in this business and any other business if you truly want to succeed. To actually get to talk to, learn from, and be around these people is an awesome experience.

So, the first thing I did after getting my license was to join a well-known national real estate training company. I listened to the tapes and competed every week with the people in the office that were on the same program. My production went straight up compared to other agents that decided not to follow this route.

I quickly became the top agent in my office. I was so glad that I made this life changing decision because someone once told me, "Tom, in order for you to make a million, you first need to become the person that can make the million". He was so right!

When you find a trainer, get one that is on your side and lets you make your own mistakes. This is where your own passion comes from. What kind of dreams and goals do you have? What are your core beliefs? Do you want to be another Mother Theresa in life and just help people all day long? You could give all the money that you make away. Great! Don't laugh; I know people who do this in real estate and they are very successful at it. They are very happy, too. These are the people that actually inspire me, because they are very selfless. I said self*less* not selfish! They think of others first, then think of themselves.

My wife and I are at the point and stage of mass contribution in life right now and let me tell you how good it feels to do this.

Remember, we are dead a lot longer than we are alive – unless we leave behind an inspiration and legacy that will live through others! So while you are here living, why not become outstanding, not just great at what you do so you not only inspire people, but also empower them!

In the past, I was able learn from my own experience of hiring the right trainer. Trainers are not cheap, but you definitely get what you pay for…and more! If you hire one on the pretense that they will make you a lot of money in a short period, then you are in a fog. If you hire someone knowing that you yourself have to go through all the motions and learning experiences in life and actually expect that it will take a lot more time than previously imagined, then you are on the right track.

Interviewing the right trainer

Here are some very important starter questions to ask when interviewing for a potential trainer.

1. How long have you been in the business or industry?
2. What type of prospecting do you like to teach? FSBO's, Expired's, Past Clients? Or is it all by referral only?
3. How do you train? Is there a specific plan that you follow week by week?

Call and talk to several trainers, and you will find after hanging up the phone with them that some of these companies are just not a right fit for you. It's not just about whether you personally like them or not. It's about what you can learn from them and how they can support you; then eventually you will pass it on. It's how you can learn from their mistakes and have them relate to you in their own past experiences.

Getting into real estate can and will change your life. If you want it to, it will become the most rewarding experience in your life. In some of the following chapters, I will share my dilemmas, my defeats and, of course, my successes. I hope that you will learn from them, but also know that there is no magic pill that you can take to have the life of your dreams. It is in you to work hard and smart. So, in sum, "Go out and learn today!"

The New Age Real Estate Agent

Chapter 2

The Power of Attraction

"The most important thing is to be whatever you are without shame."

Rod Steiger

All the great minds in this world have known of the power of attraction. What you put out there will always come back to you. Whether it is negative energy or positive, it never fails to come back to you. It also never fails to keep traveling from the point of origin.

I always ask myself this question on a continual basis; what am I passionate about in my life right now?

Why am I here?

The answers have always been the same. Because I want to be the best, I can be with the resources that either are given to me or mine for the taking. I only live life once, so why not make the very best of it every single day that I am alive. I do not want to be on my deathbed and wishing that I could have made a difference in life to me and others I touched.

The New Age Real Estate Agent

Tuning in

The power of attraction is like a radio signal. You turn the dial until you get in tune with a certain signal you match up with. There are certain frequencies that you are attracted to and that you attract.

It's like this – if you love rock and roll, your patterns are to pick up mostly on rock and roll stations. On the other hand, if you like classical, then the same holds true. Now think of the person that knows of several different stations of different varieties. This person is in tune with more than just the guy that only tunes into rock and roll.

It's like seeing the homeless person on the street waving his hands and ghost punching something. He is only in tune with that one negative station and cannot get off of it. If you focus your frequencies to love and harmony in your life, then that's what you will attract.

So What Are You Thinking About Most?

Whatever you are focused on right now is like planting a seed for a tree. When you first have a thought, no matter if it is negative or powerful, you plant a seed under the surface of the ground. The more you think about it, the more it grows under the surface. The funny thing is that you can't see it yet, but it is there growing and growing.

With this in mind, can you see why there are so many failed realtors, so much road rage in our society today? Take the married couple, for example – why is it that consistently 50% keep failing? Is it because 50% of those couples keep focusing on the negative and what they are not getting out of the relationship?

What if these couples took a different view on the matter and focused their energy to positive and empowering thoughts and desires? What if they hung out with other powerful couples and surrounded their relationships with all positive energy – like going to great seminar classes on relationships, even if they don't need it – don't you think it would do them good?
I have found that there is either love or fear in a relationship, the two cannot co-exist at the same time. With my relationship with my wife, we always have to come from a foundation of love and contribution. If there is any fear, jealousy or negativity involved in communications, then it either will not work out or it will take longer. The reason it will take longer is because we will soon figure out that it was based on fear and not our foundation of love and contribution.

If you truly want to be an outstanding agent, then you need to focus 100% on achieving the things you want your business to be like and meditate on those things only.

The seed was planted with the married couple, they fell in love, said their vows, and expected to just float along and everything would be OK. Unbeknownst to them that when they planted the seed and it started growing, they gave up just when the bud started coming out of the surface. A lot of people let the bud die and go on to plant another seed, which they think is way more easier then actually working on their commitment to marriage.

Likewise, the normal real estate agent that plants their seed never even sees a bud come out of the ground. They give up way before it reaches the surface. So it dies and they blame that there was not enough water that year or sunlight to nurture the seed, never taking responsibility for planting it in the first place.

How To Make It Work For Your Benefit

You must be in harmony with what you desire in the first place, because if you are not then it will take much longer to happen. It's just like when someone listens to rock and roll for years and then someone says to them, "Hey, you have to hear this new music! Turn your dial to 106.4 – it will make you a lot of money!" So they reluctantly turn their dial to 106.4 in hopes to make some money and have a better life, but it turns out to be a classical station, which just goes all against every cell in their body. Now if they decide to at least give it a try, they turn on the law of attraction. They are not in harmony with it at first, but they are willing to give it a try knowing what it will give them.

When someone is being true to themselves, focusing on the things they like and at the same time bringing good feelings, then they will get what they desire much faster. Not to say you cannot get what you desire, but if you are like the person who dislikes classical music and are willing to give it a try, then the bud will soon grow, it will just take longer and this is something they have to realize and accept.

Of course, it comes even faster when your whole body accepts what you desire because you are putting feeling into it. This is why negative emotions and negative self-talk do not work, because you are actually pushing away that which you desire. So when you understand the law of attraction, you realize that everything comes to you because you attract it to yourself.

The New Age Real Estate Agent

If you are a top-producing realtor, then you attracted that to yourself. If you are a realtor struggling along in hopes that it will get better, then you attracted that, too.

By knowing this, it makes things much easier to accept. Especially when failure happens, you know that you are not in tune and do not deserve it yet, but soon will. If you live paycheck to paycheck and would like to turn that around, then do something different. Focus on having an unlimited supply of money and financial freedom. By focusing on having to come up with a certain amount per month, then that's what you will get – only a certain amount!

Start by respecting your money and appreciating it in your wallet or purse. Don't just throw the bills all crumpled up in there; fold them nicely and treat them with the respect they deserve. For the person who treats his money without respect has none.

There is no limit to the amount of money you can have; the only limits are the ones you put on yourself and the limits of how much you deserve. It is a little hard to think this way at first, but with practice you will get better and better. Who knows, but maybe this is the rest of our 90% human potential that we have not tapped into yet.

I remember when I was younger and I had this type of thinking introduced to me. It was a very hard concept to grasp at first, but I would always know the outcome. Of course, hanging around people that do not think this way only makes it harder, because they do not want to lose the rapport they have with you. At first you feel really weird because it goes against the natural way you think. It seems like you are focusing on your emotions, what you say and what you think all the time, and it can get stressful. This is why to make it easier you need to surround yourself with others that think like this (positively), and with books that communicate like this. Not only that, but get rid of the negative influences in your life like the TV and newspaper. By doing that, it makes things so much easier to do what you have and must do in life to get to where you want to be. It is always going to be something that you are mastering in life...this is the key to a successful and fulfilling life!

If you are reading this and have been a struggling realtor for some time now, then maybe it is time you realized this is not worth it for you and now you can spend your energy on something that makes you truly happy. Or you can realize the power of attraction and know that you just needed to redirect your energy on things that you like to do more, like door knocking or more of a referral-based business. But whatever you do, do <u>something</u> and take responsibility for your actions.

Practice also the art of gratitude. Thank everyone for everything that you have in your life now. By doing this, you not only focus on the positive and naturally attract more, but you are also allowing things to happen as well. Too many of us get something and feel that this is what is deserved to us with an ego. But by letting go of your ego and allowing it to happen with gratitude, it will come more freely and be accepted by all the cells in your body.

Looking Forward and Setting Goals

Imagine what you'd like your life to be like in every area, sit down with a pencil and paper and answer the following questions.

1)   What do I want my life to be like in three years? In

five years? In 20 years?

2) How much money will I be earning then? Is the sky the limit?

3) What does my family look like? Are they a group of strong individuals with lots of self-esteem? Am I proud of them? Are they proud of me? Do we do things together and have an exciting, fulfilling life?

4) How big of a house do we live in? Does it matter?

5) How many rental properties do we own?

6) Do we have a positive cash flow?

7) Am I learning new things in life like the piano or oil painting or bike racing?

8) Is my life less stressful because of the person I have become?

9) What does my health look like? Am I the poster child for, "We fry 'em. you eat 'em" or the poster child for a health magazine with my muscles on fire?

Then make up more of your own custom questions that will really drive you to get out of bed early every single day and be excited about life and let the power of attraction work.

I remember at first, my goals were so small compared to now. I just wanted to make a lot of money, thinking that by doing that all the things in life that I wanted would magically appear. **It does not work that way.**

You need to become a better person in life before things happen your way on a consistent basis. Did you get that? Of course, there are people out there making a lot of money. There are even lottery winners that make it every single day. But what happens to most of those people? They lose it! They are not

The New Age Real Estate Agent

worthy of having it in the first place. **So first, you need to become the person worthy of making the million, before you can make the million.**

Having a dream and putting it in writing every day and focusing on it will be the reason that drives you daily. If you are single, start by writing out who your next mate will be, such as:
Brunette
Medium build
Not grossly thin like a super model, but healthy
Certain age
Attractive
Beautiful, flowing hair
Smart
Soft spoken
Smiles all the time
Speaks several languages
Always dresses nicely
Wants to be a lifetime learner
And so on...

Practicing such affirmations, reading good books, and meditating are the best way to keep your focus daily. Here is an example of my daily affirmations that I write out every morning when I get to the office:
I am a calm person.
A lot of money flows through me daily. (Get that? "Flows through" meaning I have mass inflow and help others, too.)
I smile a lot.
I am confident.

The New Age Real Estate Agent

I am a great leader.
I have a great wife and family.
I listen.
I give more than I take; I am a giving person.
I have high integrity with myself and others.
I exercise daily with intensity.
I eat healthy food.
I play the piano with passion and have fun.
I am a great tri-athlete.
I am a lifetime learner.
This book is a best seller that helps millions of
     agents and business owners.

As of the time of writing this book, these are my daily affirmations. Ten years ago when I started writing them, they were nothing like that. But that's OK, because I had to start somewhere.

The funny thing about writing affirmations is that they always come true after awhile; this is part of the power of attraction. I remember re-reading some that I had saved from years before and I was shocked that every single one of them had come true.

Like Napoleon Hill's book, *Think and Grow Rich*, says, "What man can conceive and believe, so can he achieve." I encourage you to read this book, as well as What to Say When You Talk to Yourself by Shad Helmstetter. Both will teach you about affirmations and positive self-talk. Another good one is Ask and It Is Given by Esther and Jerry Hicks.

I have a new way of committing to my affirmations daily. While writing them out, I also memorize them in a song format, too. By memorizing them in a song, I can take them with me anywhere.

All I need is within me now, I pray for God's will to be done somehow. When speaking to people everywhere, they say I'm passionate, funny and that I care. Honesty, integrity are the games for me, I have perfect health, as you can see. I live with passion and teach others, too, cause life without it is just too blue.

I love and trust my family oh so much, we call ourselves the Hale bunch. My purpose in life is to help others grow, I'm totally committed - don't you know?

Your dreams and goals will always be changing throughout your life, so accept and get use to this. The trick is to know when you are getting too comfortable with things. You need to always be asking yourself some important questions throughout life. These are the questions I ask myself:

1) Have I achieved my goals?
2) Do I really like my goals and am I truly motivated to achieve them?
3) Are my goals someone else's or are they mine?
4) Should I sit down and write out some new goals?

By doing this exercise on a consistent basis, you will see that you are human and you will get tired with things on a continual basis. The best advice I can give you is to not make the reason why you are doing this an amount of money that you <u>need</u> to earn. Don't get me wrong – I think you need to have that in your goals, but it shouldn't be the only reason.

Listen to the word, "need." Is there any giving with that? No.

Let me give you an example of what I mean. For years, I had always set a dollar amount of income that I wanted to have for the next year – 100k, 200k, 400k, 600k, 1 million and so on.

The New Age Real Estate Agent

There came a time when the money did not motivate me anymore. Now I mean motivate me in the sense of waking up when I have to and doing the things I do or don't want to in order to achieve that goal. In other words, I think complacency will set in a lot faster with you if your only goals are to make a lot of money.

Conversely, your mind will grow and expand if you let it and your thinking will get bigger every year.

How My Own Thinking Progressed

My own life is a great example of the law of attraction. Some of my earliest goal setting started when I used to watch the circus clowns on their one-wheeled bikes (unicycle) when I was younger and be amazed that they could do such a feat. I wanted so badly to learn how to do this, but never even bothered to tell my parents. So, I never bothered to ask or communicate that to them.

So when I was eight years old, my dad worked at Sears Roebuck. One night he brought a unicycle home from work and said, "Hey kids, I just got this at a great price. Anyone want to learn to ride it?" as he held it up. I didn't even think twice about it and said, "Yeah! I'll do it!" So for the next two months everyday, I came home from school and propped myself up on the one-wheeled contraption, leaned against the garage door for support and pushed myself off. My motivation was to ride that thing no matter what! I remember the wheel used to just pop out from under me so fast that the next thing I recalled I was kissing the concrete and chipping my teeth. A lot of bruises later, I was finally able to ride it about one full turn of the wheel. How exciting! But why was I so determined to do such a skyscraper feat at the young age of eight?

Did the power of attraction have everything to do with it? Was it because I focused on it day and night and even missed dinner a number of nights? Why would such a young kid be so determined to accomplish this?

I can finally understand it now as I am older. It <u>was</u> because of the law of attraction. Since I wanted this so badly, the universe set up and rewarded me with what I needed at exactly the moment I needed it.

My mom would always be supportive and tell me that I was such a determined little boy that always got what he wished for. My WWII veteran dad used to tell me, "Work hard in life and you will get anything you want." These were the people I was surrounded by – my positive affirmations, if you will, at the tender age of eight. I never told my friends what I was doing because one time I did tell one and he laughed at me. So I swore I would not tell anyone until I could actually do it and the next time they saw me was when I was on it riding circles around them!

After I was finally able to ride the unicycle further and further, one day I rode it to school and all the kids were so impressed that a third-grade teacher came out and had me ride it for his class. My passion then was to ride that unicycle all over the place, and I did. The power of attraction was well at work.

My next passion was getting my private pilot's license. When I was 16, I started flying lessons at a local airport. Knowing that I had to be 18 before I could actually get the license, I was motivated to get it and pay for it myself. I used to save enough money just for one lesson ($60 an hour then). But my goal was to get my license by my 18th birthday. When my

The New Age Real Estate Agent

18th birthday came, I did not have enough hours and training for the final exam, but I kept on pushing. I even got a job at the local airport refueling and washing planes just so I could be closer to my goal.

Then the worse thing in my life happened, my father got ill and was told he had six months to live. He had cardiomyopathy (a weak valve in his heart). It was a very hard time for the family because we all watched this strong man slowly wither away and lose more and more weight everyday. Since they told him he had only six months to live, he never talked about it once with any of us, which I guess was good for him because it seemed like he was not focusing on it and therefore prolonged the conclusion. He lived for two years after the doctor told him the news and it was the longest two years of my life. The whole family was walking on eggshells trying to keep peace in the house, and it worked. But the toll it took on the family was much worse because we all kept everything inside – the pain and even the happiness for fear of feeling too overconfident in his presence.

One day I can remember very vividly. We were sitting in the living room, he was in a robe and watching the famous soap Luke and Laura (he would never admit that to me) and he told me two wishes that he had before he died and they were, "Take care of your mother," and "Spread my ashes over the countryside where I grew up in a plane that you are flying." This was the last discussion we had together and it seems like yesterday. So this naturally made me push even harder to achieve my goal of getting my license.

So after he passed away, I received my pilot's license and I spread his ashes over the countryside with my mom and sisters in the plane with me. It was a very sad, eerie, yet proud feeling,

The New Age Real Estate Agent

to say the least. It was hard to deal with all the different emotions at the time for me. I experienced joy because of the achievement of my pilot's license. I experienced sadness for my father's death. I experienced gratitude that I was fulfilling his wish. I experienced the peace of his spirit within me and how proud he was of me. I experienced the emotions my mom and sisters went through while riding in the plane with me. It was an experience that I will never forget and it definitely made me stronger.

At the college I attended at the time, I studied for the degree of aviation professional pilot. I soon received that degree, but had no passion to become a commercial pilot. I could not see myself being tied down and staring at the same thing all day. So I went to a Navy recruiter and tried to get into OTS (Officer Training School) so I could fly fighter jets. I was not accepted because I did not have 20/20 uncorrected vision. Of course, the Navy tried to sell me on having a different career, but I knew what I wanted and did not want, so therefore I lost my passion for flying.

A few years ago, I had Lasik eye surgery done on both eyes to better them to 20/20 vision – what timing! Oh well, all for the better because now you have in your hands a great book to show you the way to a successful real estate career!

I had a best friend at the time who worked at the airport with me fueling planes. We also went to the same college for the same degree in aviation. We had a lot in common because his mom had died when he was younger and he knew how I felt about my father's death.
He wanted to fly for a major airline and be a captain of a 747 someday. The power of attraction was working with him.

I did a lot of thinking on that as my career too, but after seeing many deaths of pilots that I knew at the airport, I slowly changed my mind. I don't care how alive I felt when I was in the air; no great feeling will stop a plane from crashing. So unless I could have been in the cockpit of an F-16 fighter, I would not have taken that chance back then. So now I fly for recreational purposes and have a lot of fun with all the new high tech avionics such as GPS. The good news is that I have my private pilot's license for life and get to use it whenever and however I want.

My friend did finally achieve his goal and now works for a major airline. I feel he looks at me as kind of lucky in the sense that I did not have to jump through all the hoops in life and all the long, boring flight hours to be wealthy and happy. I almost feel guilty for it, but this is life and the power of attraction. I knew it was not for me, so I used my common sense and it came out to my advantage.

My next passion in life was when I moved to Los Angeles from Portland. It was after my father passed away and I just wanted to bust out of my hometown. So I went soul searching to find out what I really wanted in life at that time – where I fit in. I worked some odd jobs in warehouses here and there and experienced a few earthquakes, and then it finally hit me. I must have gotten so used to looking at all the brown landscape in southern California that I got homesick for the green of Oregon and wanted to come home to snow ski. (California is a beautiful state!)

So I called up a ski resort to see if they needed any ski instructors and they said, "Yes, we will even train you for free, with a free seasons pass, too!" I was there in two days. They trained me and I had a great time meeting some really cool people and being a ski bum at the same time. I taught kids, grown-ups, college students and even blind people (yes, blind people). I knew in my heart I was living life to the fullest because

The New Age Real Estate Agent

I was experiencing so many things and meeting so many different types of people, too.

I had a passion in my heart to be the best ski instructor on the mountain and to gain that great experience. I used to go down the face (double black diamond) with no poles! I did it just to push myself to get better. People on the chairlift above looking down thought I was nuts.

I used to drop one ski at the beginning of the lift when I got on and ski all the way down on one ski, then change feet at the bottom and do it again, just so I could get better. And since I was up there all day long skiing, I naturally got better. I remember one time I had a couple of my weekend warrior friends come up and spend the day with me and I thought I would give them a good scare. So I took off as we got off the chairlift and yelled behind me to them, "Come on guys, follow me!" as my voice grew softer going down the hill. I went way ahead of them and took down the double black diamond signs without them seeing. They followed and tried to keep up as fast as they could on the perfect, powdery day. They were behind me about 20 feet going around 35 mph on a flat spot and from their perspective they saw me vanish down the mountain in front of them. Then I looked up and there they came down screaming at the top of their lungs.

What had happened was I went off a 25-foot cliff and they did too. The landing could have not been more perfect, with about two feet of fresh, powdery snow, so I knew they would be alright. If I had done it any other way, they would not have had that experience with me. They were so happy and mad at me at the same time, but later said it was a great experience and thanked me for it. Sometimes people just need a little push in life – when you know they're up for it…and ready.

The New Age Real Estate Agent

I taught a lot of people how to ski and one of the best experiences was teaching the blind. I had to ski backwards while they totally – and I mean totally – trusted me. I would say, "right" or "left" or "slow" and "stop" to guide them. It was very hard at first, but when I saw the joy on their faces, it was a very magical feeling. Picture a blind person on skis coming down a hill laughing and having so much fun. It is a very humbling experience. These people had never experienced this before and I was proud to introduce it to them. They liked coming to me because they told me that they liked the confidence in my voice and the calmness about me.

So when I was skiing, I met group of people that skied in the winter and windsurfed in the summer in the Columbia River Gorge (between Oregon and Washington). What a great life to live, I thought...which brought me to my next passion.

I moved to Hood River, Oregon, from the mountain in the spring time so I could be closer to windsurfing. Hood River back then was considered the windsurf capital of the world. I hung out with a group of guys that had the same dream as I did – **nothing** but having fun!

The ski season was over and it was time to start sailing (windsurfing). So I called up a skiing buddy that owned a windsurf shop and anxiously asked for a lesson. He told me that the water was too cold now and that I should call in another month. Another month!! I couldn't wait another month; I wanted to do it now!

I did not have a job, so I applied at the local bar to help out serving beer and drinks. This is where all the action was for the boardheads (windsurfers) and I got to know even more of them. I hardly made any money from the tips there, though, and could not afford to pay for windsurfing lessons. I told this to my

The New Age Real Estate Agent

friend that was the owner of the windsurf shop and he said, "Well, I do need the toilets cleaned." So guess what I was doing at 6 a.m. every morning? But then, guess what I was doing every afternoon? I was sailing – and getting damned good at it, too. By the end of the summer, I was as good as or better than some of the veterans that sailed for years. I also gained their respect, too.

Most of us had went to college and had normal lives before that, but just wanted to truly experience life in a different way. So we set up our lives where we could live on about 10k a year to get by. Nothing mattered except where the wind was going to blow that day. We would chase wind for hours to find it and finally get our rush only to look forward to the next day. We would go to Baja California in the winter and hang out on the Pacific side windsurfing and having a great time. When we ran out of food, we would trade beer or used clothing to the local Mexican fisherman for lobster and fish.

By living my passion then, it led me to wanting to support myself in this way of life. So I opened up my own windsurfing business and manufactured booms (the part you hold onto when windsurfing that goes around the sail). I ended up even inventing a small-diameter grip for women that was very strong to hold up to the Gorge winds. The old style boom was a thick girth and even men with smaller hands had a hard time hanging on. And when you are out sailing in 40 knots of wind, the last thing you want to worry about is your hands cramping up on you or the boom breaking and leaving you in the middle of the Columbia River floating downstream and something bad happening to you.

So my super strong, small-diameter boom was a hot seller and I could not make them fast enough. People came to my shop and bought my booms knowing that they could be safe and have a trendy product.

The New Age Real Estate Agent

And after a particularly messy incident windsurfing one day on the Gorge, after which my friends dubbed me, "Mast Head Roy," (after my middle name, Roy, and getting hit over the head with a mast), I even found the perfect mascot to brand my products with, helping them take off like wildfire.

Mast Head Roy was an instant success! People from all over could not get enough of him – T-shirts, stickers, sail stickers, and even a weekly article that he wrote in the local windsurf magazine. I put Mast Head Roy's image (drawn by me) on my booms and called them Booms From Hale. What a great product that people wanted to be a part of, because it was fun and exciting! I did radio and TV commercials, not to mention all the magazine publicity. I got calls from all over the world for stickers and anything with Mast Head Roy. After that, it was a lot easier to sell my booms and run a profitable business (and perhaps my first lesson at the value of logos and branding, which I talk more about related to real estate in chapter 5).

So the power of attraction was at full force for me then. Did I get hit over the head for a reason? Was it some terrible thing I did in the past or was it just the energy I was putting out there to have a successful company?

You can also look at this situation from a different perspective and know that when something happens to you, whether good or bad, you have the power to decide what you can do with that energy to turn it into something good. The things that come your way are limitless only if you come from a point of giving and helping people fulfill their dreams and being grateful to them at the same time.

So what a great life! I had just enough money coming in to support my dream, which was to windsurf and have a successful company. It all came together and it was very rewarding living life like this, being able to sail and live for the wind!

The power of attraction was with me the whole time because I was so focused on living life to the fullest everyday on the least amount of money. And since I knew that and believed in that, that is what I received!

Living that lifestyle after about three years, I got complacent and wanted to make more money to be able to live in a nice home and "have it all," so I thought to myself, "What do people have to have but costs a lot of money?" My answer was real estate! I got my license and started selling.

At first, the power of attraction was not working because I hated it. I hated looking out the window of the real estate office and seeing all the cars go by with windsurfing boards on top. I hated being tied down and not free to do what I wanted. It was a perfect example of how the power of attraction will not work if you are not into it. Just because you are committed to something – and I thought I was because I was a cold-calling fool – the power of attraction will not work to its fullest.

After about eight to nine years of what I call struggling, it finally hit me over the head (again!). I was so into trying to sell real estate the way they teach you. Well, the way they teach you is to be a normal realtor and just get by. I finally said to myself, "I am going to write out a plan and trust the power of attraction like I did all the years before with different dreams." Trust your gut! And after about two years of trusting my gut, I tripled my business and had a way more rewarding life!

So now some of my daily passions at this stage in life include oil painting, piano, racing my bicycle, ballroom dancing with my wife, competing in

The New Age Real Estate Agent

triathlons and being a leader for my family by helping them be the best they can be. The kids are taking tae- kwon-do, learning piano, basketball, football and other things they enjoy. But the biggest thing that I can help them with – just like a good coach would do – is to believe in them and let them make their own mistakes and at the same time, have them be <u>responsible</u> for all their actions.

When you are responsible for your own actions, you learn faster and it makes you a better person at the same time. You are less dependent on others because it increases your self-esteem.

It's funny that I think that these passions that I do today are going to last until the day I die. But looking back on the history of how I've lived, these are just more drops in the bucket of my exciting life. It could be that way for yours, too, if you just open your heart and do the things you want to do and trust the power of attraction. Because life is way too short.

The New Age Real Estate Agent

Chapter 3

For Sale By Owners and Expired Listings

"If we had no winter the spring would not be so pleasant; if we did not sometimes taste adversity, prosperity would not be so welcome."
Anne Bradstreet

For sale by owners and expired listings are a great source of income. But the trick is to not get addicted to them. What do I mean by getting addicted to them? I mean having your whole business be dependent on the them. If you are dependent on them, then you are giving them power and control over your business.

Expired Listings

First of all, let's tackle the expireds and answer a few questions.

Who are they? They are listings that were on the market and never sold. Why did they not sell? That is your job to find out by asking a lot of questions. But in most cases, it was because the price was too high and the market was not willing to pay that certain price for it.

A good way to look at expireds is to know that they expired for a *reason*. Whatever the reason is for you to find out and solve it. A lot of times, it was not only because the price was too high, but the agent never communicated with the seller on a professional basis to adjust the price. I have known a lot of agents that take a listing and then just sit on it and never communicate with the sellers. The seller needs to know what is going on with their listing. This is why they hired an agent in the first place, because they could not do it on their own or just simply do not want to do it on their own.

Expireds can range anywhere from people that are overbearing to the shyest mouse. But, in most cases, it is the agent's fault for it expiring in the first place.

Why did the agent take an overpriced listing? Why did the agent not have the skills to overcome an overbearing person that wanted to be in control? Even if they were not overbearing, why didn't the agent communicate with the seller? If you are not the type of agent that has the skills to handle these people, then I suggest you leave them to the rest of the agents that can, so you don't waste everyone's time.

If it was a shy agent that just happened to have a listing fall in their lap, then where were that agent's skills in pricing it correctly in the first place?

If you are in real estate sales and want to be a top-listing agent, then you better get comfortable with telling the truth to people, even if it hurts and may potentially lead to not getting the listing or doing any business with them. You need to be very good at pricing homes appropriately, because you never want to have a listing expire. Rather than that, you should always cancel the listing or give it back to the seller if you can't agree on the price and terms.

This is one reason why I have all my appointments come into the office. I am in control and if and when I get the person that wants to do it their way or the highway, then I just do not deal with them and leave them for the agents that want anything thrown at them.

With that said, listing up expireds is really quite simple. It's all mindset and how you view the whole situation. The following points are particularly key:

- Be the first one to call and set an appointment.
- Ask a lot of questions as to why their listing expired.
- Qualify them to see if you even want the listing.
- Set an appointment to meet.
- Or list them over the phone.

When you are the first one to call them, they are more open to talking to you. Think of the person that had her house on the market, nothing happened, and they got really frustrated. Then the night before it expired, they were in a real fix not knowing what to do. Then you call first thing in the morning and really care to know what happened. By doing this, you will get the listing the majority of the time – if you really want it.

In order to qualify them and find out if you really want

the listing, however, you need to ask three important questions:
- Why?
- Where?
- When?

Why Are They Moving?

Did they already buy another house and it closes soon? Do they really *want* to move? What is their motivation?

Where Are They Moving To?

Do they have definite plans and a real motivation to move?

When Are They Moving?

Do they have a specific time that they are moving?

By answering these three most important questions, you can get them pre-qualified to see if you even want to take the listing.

If the answer to, "Why are you moving?" is, "Oh, we just thought we could put the house up for sale, and if we move, we move, and if we don't, then we don't," get off the phone right away and don't waste your or their time!

For further ideas at approaching expireds, you can start off with a script like below, but be aware that you have to make it your own so you can feel comfortable using it.

The New Age Real Estate Agent

Sample Expireds Script

Good morning! This is Jon Doe with ABC Realty. How are you today? Great!

It looks like your contract expired on the MLS today, is that correct? Oh, I'm so sorry it did not sell.

Why are you moving?

Where are you moving to?

When do you have to be there?

Was your home shown much when it was on the market?

Well, the great news is that I am the expert on selling homes in the area (*once you are, then you can say this; if not, delete this line or modify to a "top Realtor in the area"*) **and I was curious if I could take 10 minutes of your time to show you why your property did not sell. Do you have time this afternoon at 2 p.m. or would 4 p.m. be better? I don't mind putting you in my schedule at that time.**

This expired script works well for me, although you might want to change it to fit you and your style.
Remember about the power of attraction and if you really do not like expireds, then it will take a lot longer then you think. Or you may not want to even touch them. But if you are like me – and I like a challenge – then you will take them on and use them as a stepping stone before you own your market.

The trick with expireds is to have them sell as fast as you can. Do not leave them on the market at a high price for very long. These people sometimes get complacent and think that because their home did not sell fast the last time, that this time will be the same and it should not sell too fast again either.

The New Age Real Estate Agent

I always used the power of attraction with all of my sellers. I say, "I need you both to focus on and visualize your home selling fast, can you do that?" Then they say, "Of course, anything you say, Tom."

The point is, you have to do something radically different from the last agent (like price it right) and take control so it will allow itself to sell. By allowing it to sell, I mean set it up so that it does and the buyer comes in at the right time with an offer.

For Sale By Owners (FSBOs)

Have you yourself never tried to sell something on your own? And can you blame some of these FSBOs for doing it in the first place? They have to talk to some of these greedy agents that don't even realize why they are selling homes in the first place! But they do know they want the FSBOs' money! How ironic it is and no wonder why most agents fail after 18 months in the business. They just don't have a plan or, worse yet, it's the person that they are.

So the FSBO is a little different then the expired. They need to see that they can or cannot do it on their own. Sometimes they are just not motivated either. So you need to ask a lot of pre-qualifying questions before you take their listing. Questions like:

Where are you moving to?

Why are you moving?

When are you moving?

Figure out their motivation, just like the expired. Here is a powerful script that I used.

The New Age Real Estate Agent

Sample FSBO Script

Hello, my name is Tom Hale with The Hale Group Real Estate. How are you today? Great!

I see that you are trying to sell your home on your own. Any luck yet? No? Oh well, I'm sure it will happen sooner or later.

I'm just curious, where are you moving to?

Why are you moving?

When are you moving there?

Have you had any bites on your home yet?

Do you think your home will take long to sell in this market?

Have you ever sold a home on your own yet?

I am thinking your selling on your own is to save on commission, is that right or is there another reason?

Well, I am the expert in the area – have you seen all my signs? Especially the ones with SOLDS on them?

I know you are selling on your own and I will be in the area on my way home. What I will do is drop of a pack of information on your door in case you might want a few tips on selling your home in today's market. Does that sound good?

And if you ever need any advice from the top agent in the area, don't hesitate to call me!

Now, let's look at the script. There are many different ways to go about talking to FSBOs. The point I am making here is to just call and visit them no matter what. It is a lot more then what other agents are doing. FSBOs and expireds need to have a feeling of trust before they will list with you. There are some trainers out there that train you to go for the throat and jugular, but I disagree. I want to earn their respect and have the power of attraction working for me so I can get more referrals from them. If you do a great job and sell their home quickly, then they will refer a lot of people to you.

To list up FSBOs, you have to be consistently aggressive. What do I mean by that? I mean that you have to keep in front of them at all times, so when they do decide to list, you will be on their mind. I would list them after seeing them anywhere from one to eight times. On average, it was about five times that I was in contact with them before I took the listing. I have also found the best times to call them or visit them face to face is on Mondays. This day is perfect because they did not sell their home on their open house the day before on Sunday and might just be in the mood to talk to you.

The next thing to address is your commission and getting paid. There are a lot of agents out there that just go for the FSBOs and have a commission cutting system in place for them. I have even seen agents do it for free because they sold them a home and would get that commission from that house selling. All I can say is these agent have no guts, no dignity, no class and no integrity with themselves or other agents. They just don't get it. They do not realize that we are all in this together, and so what one agent does affects the rest of us. These agents were never trained by the best, so they know no different.
It's agents like you and I that stand to our word and get better no matter what, and those agents end up taking the crumbs of our glory.

So why do agents cut their commissions? No training? Personality? Greed? They <u>have</u> to have a listing so they can get an award as top listing agent for the month? These are all correct answers, but the real reason is that they have no goals and reason why they are doing all of this. If they had a real reason why, a real reason that was honorable and pushed them to grow to new heights, then they would be more mature and see what they were doing.

You can't blame it on the FSBO; this is the reason they are doing it in the first place! So it is all the agent's responsibility to not cut their commission.

But no, the agents that are out there on a consistent basis cutting their commission, it's all about them and they need to take care of themselves before doing something as radical as having self-respect and a kinship to their business associates.

So here is a great response to the FSBO that wants you to cut your commission. (Of course, first of all, I encourage you to ask them why they would ask in the first place.)

FSBO: How much commission do you charge?

Me: The normal 6 or 7 percent

FSBO: There is no way I would pay that amount.

Me: Great, but if your house could sell faster with less problems, and maybe even more in your pocket, would you at least listen to what I had to say?

FSBO: Maybe.

Me: Great, I will see you tonight at 4 p.m.

Then just show them that someone always loses when commissions are cut and the FSBO never wants to see a loss. Show them that by cutting a commission, it will appear as such in the MLS and very good agents often only show homes that are priced right and have a good to great buyer's agent commission to be paid. If they want a top agent showing their house, then they need to keep the commission up to normal or higher. I say higher because there will be less problems when a buyer's agent sees that they will be getting paid more, so they will not rock the boat and instigate a sale fail. Obviously, this thinking and mindset should be used whether or not you are in front of a FSBO.

Objection Handlers

Over the years, I've developed some very useful answers to the many objections that come from expireds and FSBOs. Here are a few:

-We want to think about it. This just means that you had a poor presentation, so I advise you to get better then you will never hear it again. Find out what the real objection is by asking more questions at this time.

-We have a friend that we will use. If their friend was so good in the first place, then why didn't they use them?
Me: I can appreciate that and most people do have a friend in the business, but let me ask you this. Is this one of your most important assets that you own?
Them: *Yes.*
Me: So even though you have a friend, wouldn't it make sense to at least get a second opinion about the price and marketing?
Them: *Well, yes!*

By using a great pre-qualification script, you weed out a lot of the objections to begin with. This will let you know and decide to work with them or not. Remember, you are in control, not them. It is you that puts in long hours of studying the market and selling homes. It is you that pays your dues, not them. So be in control and certain that you are a great agent.

The most important thing to remember is that the more objections you get on a continual basis, the worse you are as an agent. Sorry for saying that, but it is the truth and I don't feel I would be writing a good book if I was not honest with you.

When you own your own market, you just do not get any objections – only *circumstances* that you have to get through. People come into my office and they are already sold on me and it is the best feeling not to have to do all the mumbo jumbo of seeing what type of person they are like a lot of the trainers teach you. It's all a bunch of horse doo-doo, and this is why you get hooked on having to go to these big seminars with the almighty great speaker that has never sold any homes except for the year they did then quit.

So again, if you are getting objections, it just means that they do not trust you and do not see you as the area expert. Or they just do not see the benefit of giving up control.

Remember that FSBO's and Expireds are good ways to get the pump primed and the money flowing in. But only use these to get you to where you want to be, and that is owning your own market. Which brings me to my next chapter...

The New Age Real Estate Agent

Chapter 4

Finding, Targeting, and Capturing a Market

"To focus on the target is the same as hitting it - just pull back and let go, then do it again."
                                        Tom Hale

Focusing on an area to target and capture can be done a number of different ways. The first way is to ask yourself what your goals are, because if you don't know this question, then you might as well not even start.

This question has to do with personal and business goals, because if you ask me, both are tied together no matter what you think. So ask yourself, where do you want to live? Do you want to live in the best part of your town, with the nicest homes and the nicest schools for your kids? Does that matter to you? Do you need to be near a close relative or is there some other reason you want to live in a certain area? These are the first, most important questions that you need to ask yourself.

The New Age Real Estate Agent

Let me tell you a saying that fits perfect here. "If you don't have a dream, then your life will be about your problems." One more time, **"If you don't have a dream, then you life will be about your problems!"** Do you get that? Think about it really hard. When you have a dream, then all the things that come up are not problems, but stepping stones to get you to your end goal. By not having a dream, then problems come up and you have to deal with them with low energy and fear.

So in the first place, dream of the nicest town or neighborhood that you want to live in. Wherever you decide to go, by reading this book and learning what I have to say, you will and can capture the market there. What do I mean by "capture the market?" I mean become the most well-known, respected, trusted, top agent in the area that sells the most homes.

So let's say you have found the perfect town. Try to pick an area of about 2,500 to 5,000 homes and eventually get to about 10,000 homes. You need to have a lot because you need to not only think big, but have enough homes to go see on a consistent basis.

For newer agents, I would recommend picking an area of about 1,500 to 2,000 homes. But it has to have room to expand or be close to a bigger area of 7,000 to 10,000 homes. Unless, of course, you want to only keep it this size – remember, you are the boss!

Now the first thing to do is research the heck out of it by doing demographic research. Find out who lives there and why. Find out the average income per household. Find out about the schools – how many are there? How many homes does it have? Do people really want to live there or all of them moving out for some reason?

Researching a Market

A great resource for researching a market is a local title company in the area (they are likely beating down your broker's door regularly anyway, so choose one you know and trust). From a trusted title company, you can find out the following information about a market:

a) How many homes there are;
b) What the average price range of the homes per tax assessed value is;
c) What the medium income per household is;
d) How many single people per household there are;
e) How many married couples per household there are;
f) How many homes are sold per year;
g) How many expireds there were in the past year (homes that did not sell on the MLS);
h) If there is new construction;
i) Do you want to sell new construction or re-sale;
j) What the turnover rate (what percent of homes sell per year) is (you want a fast turnover rate, like say 3% to 8%);
k) What the average age of each home is.

If, after calling and asking a title company these specific questions, you don't get all your answers, then call another title company that will help you learn these things! These are the companies that you will be doing most of your closings through and they want to earn your business, so find one willing to work

The New Age Real Estate Agent

for you here.

And regarding the age of homes in a market, I have found that the statistics show that the homes between 1 to 10 years old turn over faster than the neighborhoods that are older and more established. The reason is because we live in such a disposable society that people get sick of things fast and are always looking for the newer and better things in life. The older, established neighborhoods do turn over and they are a great source, too, but if you want more listings and want to deal with newer homes, then stick to homes between 1 to 10 years old. You will have less repair issues, too, and the transactions will go a lot smoother. For example, when I first started selling in my area, I was afraid to go to the nicer areas, because I never lived in really nice homes or neighborhoods. So I sold homes all over the town, and the houses I sold were anywhere from 10 to 70 years old.

The problem with doing this was that there were many repairs on the older houses that had to be done. Issues with buried oil tanks, dry rot, mold, etc., just wreaked havoc on my business and made it very stressful. If you have 15 pendings and everyone of them has a repair issue, then it will add a lot of stress to your business. If you have 20 pendings at one time with newer construction, then you will have minimal repair issues, thus leading you to go out and find more business with less stress. Besides, you will be happier dealing with this type of a transaction, I promise.

If you need to work in a town where there are older homes and a lot of them (maybe 20,000) and not many newer homes, then research it. If there is a smaller town with more expensive homes and higher turnover, then I would go for that. Or go for both! In other words, see which area will be more profitable by working smarter, not harder.

The New Age Real Estate Agent

For example, I currently live in a good-sized city of one 2 million+ people. At the time of writing this, the average sales price in my city is only about 250k all over the board. The area that I live in and work now has about 10,000 homes, with an average price tag of about 400k. So, I could have gone out and visited the whole city (with an average price range of $250k) and it would have taken me a whole year. But then I would not have visited each home on a consistent basis. Or I could just be smart and pick the area of the newer homes that are 1 to 10 years old with a higher sales price and just visit them on a more consistent basis, like say 3 to 4 times a year.

It's easy to want it all, especially if you live in a big city! It's easy to get greedy about wanting it all, and I'll admit that that's even what I did for the longest time. I used to be the king (or so I thought) of calling expired listings in my area. I would call them first thing and get the appointment to go see them and list them up. They might have been 60 minutes away. But that was OK for me because, "I <u>needed</u> the money!"

What a disastrous way of thinking! When you come from a point of needing, you usually get what you need, but nothing more in life. What a waste of time, driving all day long on all those appointments and usually I would only take the listing 50% of the time. Not to mention, all the gas I polluted the environment with my car. But hey, I was busy being busy and it fed my ego and made me feel like I was accomplishing things.

Sounds like most people, right? I guess I had to live through that mistake on my own to learn from it. So don't make the same mistake that I did and so many other agents are doing now. Pick an area and decide now to own it! Make a commitment.

After all, what is stopping you? I'll tell you what stopped

me from that type of thinking in my early years. It was the ease of the expired listings and the ease of the FSBOs. I always thought it would be hard to capture an area and be the most respected individual there. I always thought it would take too much time and time I did not have much of, because the mortgage was due in 10 days! Let me tell you, it is a lot harder to keep on the treadmill of expireds and FSBOs then it is to capture a market. The energy one spends on thinking about owning their own market and not doing anything about it is the same energy one puts into wishing they could lose weight and never doing anything about it. It's all the same energy, so why not make a commitment and do it?

Look, don't the big companies name brand themselves? Why do they do it? Do they do it for their ego? Maybe some do, but most do not because they want to be first in the consumer's mind when thinking of real estate.

So go for it and call the expireds until you're blue in the face or get your dignity trampled on by calling some "know-it-all FSBOs." Just don't get caught up in it and become dependent on them or any other "now" business. It is real easy to do this and not break out of it. I know, I was there. Just be in control with them and know that they are a stepping stone to get you to where you want to be.

So how do you become independent from them? By coming up with a plan and committing to it. If you have money in the bank, enough to support you for the next year, then I would suggest writing a plan and following it to capture a market. Then research it like I said and start to own it.

You will own it by becoming well known there, so have the mentality that you are the area expert. Use the power of attraction and capitalize.

The New Age Real Estate Agent

Advertise in a Market to Own It

Advertise on the following in the market you want to own on a consistent basis:
-The main street bus benches
-The local grocery carts
-High school sport pamphlets
-Local fairs
-Your car
-Your shirts
-Your family's shirts
-Refrigerator magnets
-Your For Sale signs
-Mailings
-Help sponsor local events
and any other thing you can think of that will get your name out there on a consistent basis.

I started doing this with my bus benches on the main local street in my community and it works great! It takes time for the consumer to recognize my name, but can you imagine driving down a street and noticing five bus benches in a row that had the same name and logo on them? You might not think anything at first, but after a while it would become an image burned in your mind that I was the top agent that knew that area.

It is also great for new people that come into town and are driving around with real estate on their minds. They keep seeing my name and logo and, of course, I will be first on their mind to call because they see that I am the area expert – or at least I appear to be!

The New Age Real Estate Agent

So don't listen to the people that say bad things about you doing advertising and promoting yourself. They will say that you have a big ego and that you think it's all about you. Let them say it while you laugh your way to the bank! These are the people that just don't get it in life and they never will. Any successful business promotes itself if it wants to be profitable…period!

If that promotion happens to be you branding yourself, then so be it. You have to promote yourself or your business to generate income. It's the nature of the business and if you do not like doing that, then move out of the way for the people that get it. Maybe go work for someone and be dependent on their scraps that they feed you. Or face reality and get your piece of the pie now!

Some people say things like, "People want a professional," or, "You are spending way too much on that self-promotion. How can you make a profit?" My response is always the same. People list their homes and do business with me because they obviously see that I am a professional. They trust me with one of their biggest investments, don't they? It's truly fun to have the phone ring everyday with people saying they know me and want to list their homes!

The profit is an easy one to handle. I make a point to only spend 3% to 5% on my advertising and name branding…any questions? Some agents actually spend 15% to 25%! But they are doing it all the wrong way and they do not see the results.

It should be understood, of course, that all of the avenues that I listed are great, but only if you do them on a <u>consistent</u> basis. For example, the bus benches should be run for as long as you are planning to be in that area. The grocery carts can be run all the time, too, but what I do is stop them for six months and start them again in six months. Wear the T-shirts when you are at

The New Age Real Estate Agent

the grocery store or doorknocking or whenever in your community. People know that you are serious when they see you with them on all the time. And if you think you are dorky or something, then get over it or stand in the unemployment line with your trendier clothes on instead. This is a business and <u>you</u> are the business and should act like it.

I had a guy come up to me one time and say with a smile, "Tom, wherever I see you, you are always dressed like you mean business. When I go to sell my home, I am calling you, no question."

Wow! That sure beats the heck out of calling an expired and trying to prove yourself, huh?

Take responsibility and do what it takes to own your area. If it means that you will no longer be in rapport with your beer-drinking buddies at 5 p.m. or your Tupperware parties at 7 p.m., then you have to make that decision. Do you have a family that you are responsible for? Are they counting on you to help pay the bills? Do they see you as successful and a leader in the house? If so, then do what it takes and take control!

I remember when I first started advertising in my area. "It just wasn't me," I would say to myself. But then, I would look at my goals and keep the integrity with them. Where else could I have made that kind of money and be able to do the things I always wanted?

If you live in a country that will support and let you do these things to run a business, then great! If you are in America, just look at the people in the third world countries that are fighting and dieing to get here to be able to do what you are able to do! You never know how good you've had it until you lose it. We have it so easy here to be successful. But the opposite is also true – it is so easy to be spoiled and not be responsible for anything and to blame others for things not going right. It's all mindset and how you keep your nose to the grindstone. Just keep telling yourself that it is your job and nobody else's. Keep thinking of all the agents that are not willing to do what you are committing yourself to. You know the ones that drive the most expensive cars and their ego is out of control because they sold their fifth home for the year – and it's now December!

Can you see how alone you can be in this business? That's part of what this is all about. But you really aren't alone, because the few friends that you make are going to be the ones that you have something in common with – like selling homes or other business owners that want a great life. Seeing that and spending time with only the ones that really matter is how your life will be passionate. Think of spending time with your beautiful wife, husband or significant other that really respects you. They see you as a leader because you do what you say you will do. Your kids love you even more because you are able to spend time with them while you are volunteering at their schools, too. They turn out better than average because they want to be like you and start their own goals and checklists. You are their leader, their role model and their inspiration.

Using Now Business to Reach Goals

So for the rest of you that do not have the money to start your business on savings for a year, then you will have a different plan at the beginning. This is how I did it. I called the expireds and the FSBOs and got the _now_ business

The New Age Real Estate Agent

The best way to get started without a big savings account to pad your first year is to get business from the expireds, FSBOs, centers of influence, cold calling and whatever you can do to get the now business. As you are slowly making an income from these, then you need to start a process of owning an area. After some time, when you start getting recognized in that area and are comfortable not to ever call another bottom of the bucket expired or mean FSBO, then you will break away and be free to own your market for good!

How nice it is to have people call me and already trust who I am and what I represent in their own community. They call me to list their homes, to find out what the market is doing, or they call to just say hello! I don't know about you, but when the phone rings and it's someone that trusts me in selling their home and paying me a large commission, it feels good and it makes it all worthwhile because I am not only making money, but I am helping that person out. I am not fake with a script in front of me and fake being nice just because I want their listing; I take their listing and sell their home for them. This is what they want from me – an expert in their area. And I am proud to be that, knowing that I worked hard to own a market and set up a great system to succeed in that market. Which brings me to my next point…

The New Age Real Estate Agent

Chapter 5

Setting Up a Great System

"Machines are meant to run - all you need to do is maintain them every so often."

Tom Hale

Before I get started and tell you about the system, you have to ask yourself is, where do you as an agent eventually want to be in your business? Do you want to do this for the rest of your life or do you want to have the business actually run itself if you are not there? Does that sound good? Great! Then by having great systems and checklists in place, you can narrow things down to what works and what does not work. If, for instance, a sign was never put up on a new listing, then you can go to the checklist and see whose responsibility it was. If the photos taken were bad or not even done, then there is a record of whose responsibility it was.

It just makes the running of your office so much smoother and efficient to have checklists. Also, when an assistant leaves you, it makes the job that much easier to train the new assistant. Not to mention the fact if you ever get audited by the state, you can show them how efficient and prepared you are. It also makes you a real business person and frees your time up to do the most important things – like find sellers and buyers!

Assistant = Asset

If you do not have an assistant at this time, then you need to have it in your plans to get one as soon as you are selling about 25 transactions per year. That is, assuming you want to do more than 25 transactions a year.

Do not hire one if you are doing less. The reason I say this is because you are going to be busy and focused on selling homes, not wondering what kind of work you can keep your assistant busy with. Believe me, it took me a long time to get over the fact that I had to just let go and trust my assistant to do the things I had given them and know that they were working in my best interest. Sometimes the assistant did not have anything to do, but I just kept my focus on bringing in more listings and trusting that the system would soon be working.

I know of a lot of agents that hire and fire as soon as the business gets slow. But this is the wrong way to think; you have to have the mindset of getting over the hump and knowing that it is the right thing to do.

A System for Smooth, Successful Business

Setting up a system is the most important aspect of running a successful business. Setting up a plan and executing it will save you thousands of dollars and will make you less stressed and happier in the long run. And it's not rocket science to develop a system that works for you. In fact, I developed a cookie cutter system that anyone can copy and use.

Checklists Are Key

First of all, you need checklists – lots of checklists, checklists for everything! Following are some of most-used checklists:

New Listing Checklist

1a

Address:_____

Date:____ /___ /_____

Initials/Date

___ /_____   1. Install Lockbox

___ /_____   2. Enter Listing into MLS (#_____)

___ /_____   3. Fax Sign Company new order

___ /_____   4. Give listing agent a copy of MLS data for review and to approve with his initials

___ /_____   5. Take photos and download into computer

___ /_____   6. Upload photos to MLS system

___ /_____   7. Upload photos to website and make new page on website

The New Age Real Estate Agent

___/___   8. Make "New Listing" in real estate database and enter all info.

___/___   9. Put up 2-3 directional signs

___/___   10. Do a voice broadcast to 100 people in the surrounding area

___/___   11. Update "Back of all Flyers "page

___/___   12. Print final sheet for red binder

___/___   13. Hand written note to sellers- give to listing agent ready to sign and mail.

___/___   14. Head brokers initials on every page of each document.

___/___   15. Head broker to finalize this checklist

Price Reduction Checklist

2a

Address:_____

Date:_____ /___ /_____

New ML#:_____

Inititals/Date

___/____   1. Get fully signed
                "Addendum to MLS"

___/____   2. Email photos to MLS

___/____   3. Did commission change? Yes/ No
                            (Circle one)

___/____   4. Change status in database: price,
                new ML# (if there is one), enter
                notes

___/____   5. Change "Back of all flyers" to
                new price

The New Age Real Estate Agent

___/____   6. Change price on all websites

___/____   7. Call owners and tell them all is
                        complete and in order!

___/____   8. Final initials by head broker

___/____   9. File this checklist into listing file

Withdrawn or Cancellation Checklist

1c

Address:_____

Date:____/____/_____
ML#:_____

Initials/Date

___/____   1. Get fully signed "Addendum to MLS"

___/____   2. Change status on MLS to WTH or CAN

___/____   3. Delete photo and page from all websites

___/____   4. Fax sign company to remove sign

___/____   5. Change red listing folder to yellow for CAN/WTH/EXP

___/____   6. Remove photo from "Back of all Flyers"

___/____   7. Remove lockbox from property and return key to sellers

___/____   8. Call sellers and let them know of changes

___/____   9. Final initials by head broker

New Pending Checklist

1d

Address:_____

Date:____/____/_____

Initials/Date

___/____   1. Send 100 postcards surrounding property

___/____   2. Put up Pending sticker on property sign

___/____   3. Change status on MLS from Active to Pending

___/____   4. Change status in database to pending

___/____   5. Change and update all websites

___/____   6. Final initials by head broker

Expired Checklist

1e

Address:_____

Date:_____/___/_____

Initials/Date

___/____   1. Withdraw all photos and pages from websites

___/____   2. Fax sign co. to remove sign

___/____   3. Change *Red* listing file folder to _yellow_ for Canceled/Withdrawn/Expired

___/____   4. Change status in database to "Expired"

___/____   5. Remove photo from "Back of all flyers" page

___/____   6. Remove lockbox and return key to seller

___/____   7. Final initials by head broker

Sold Checklist

1f

Address:_____

Date:_____/_____/_____

Initials/Date

___/_____   1. Fax sign company to remove sign from property.

___/_____   2. Remove lockbox and give key to new sellers

___/_____   3. Change status on MLS from PEN to SLD

___/_____   4. Change status in database to "Closed and paid"

___/_____   5. Add sellers into database as "Past Clients"

___/_____   6. Final initials by head broker

Signed papers for new listing Checklist
(This goes inside the red listing file folder)

1g

Address:_____

Date:___/___/____

Listing Coordinator
    Closing Coordinator
Initials
    Initials

___/____   Disclosed Limited Agreement for
                          Sellers
    ___/____

___/____   Real estate agency disclosure pamphlet
    ___/____

___/____   Company addendum
    ___/____

___/____   Listing Contract
    ___/____

The New Age Real Estate Agent

___/___   Data input form
    ___/___

___/___   Exterior siding disclosure
    ___/___

___/___   Smoke alarm requirements addendum
    ___/___

___/___   Sellers property disclosures
    ___/___

___/___   Commission rate (What is it?) $_____
    ___/___

___/___   Processing fee? Yes/No
                           (Circle one)$___
    ___/___

Pending Sales Transaction Checklist 3a

File#_____

Date opened:_____ Estimated closing
date:_____
Property
address_____

Listing agent:_____
Selling agent:_____
Seller:_____
Buyer:_____

Initials

_____ Change status from active to pending in database
_____ Change status in MLS from active to pending
_____ Inform listing coordinator sale is pending
(Need pending or sold sticker put on sign)
_____ Closing report from database
_____ MLS property printout
_____ Sale pending letter mailed to Seller or Buyer
_____ Escrow instructions/Broker demand for real

estate commission

_____ Earnest money agreement (all pages)

     _____ Signed and dated _____ Initialed

_____ Completed by sellers/buyers/agents

_____ Contingency:_____

_____ Earnest money deposit: Note/Check

     Note dated:_____ Due:_____

     Check dated:_____

Payable to:_____

Check#_____

_____ Buyers acknowledgement on Earnest Money
agreement

_____ Sellers Counter offer   _____ Buyers
Counter offer

_____

Addendums:_____

_____ Sellers Property disclosures:_____

Exempt:_____

_____ Exterior siding disclosure:_____ New
Construction:_____

_____ Lead Base paint disclosure

_____ Oil Tank disclosure

_____ Smoke Alarm requirements

_____ Seller Agency disclosure

The New Age Real Estate Agent

_____ Buyer Agency

_____ Buyers Lender Pre-Approval letter

_____ Home inspection scheduled for: Date:_____
Time:_____

_____ Appraisal Scheduled for:
Date_____Time:_____

_____ Escrow opened with:_____
Escrow #:_____

_____ Preliminary Title report

_____ Estimated Closing statement

_____ Signing scheduled date:_____
Seller Time:_____ Buyer Time:_____

_____ Final closing HUD-1 with commission received

_____ Head Brokers initials and
date:_____

Pending Closed & Paid Checklist
(Our Listing)
3b

Property
address:_____
File #_____

List completed and initialed by: Closing coordinator and
Listing Coordinator
(Closing coordinator)

1. _____ Change status in database from pending
to closed/paid when commission check is received
in hand.

2. _____ Update sellers new forwarding address,
phone#, emails, birthdays, and   anniversaries in
database.

3. _____ Put sellers in database as "Past Clients"

4. _____ Post commission check in database and
compare to broker demand

5. _____ Attach green pending file and red
listing file together as one unit

(Listing Coordinator)

6. _____ Change MLS status from Pending to
Sold

The New Age Real Estate Agent

7. _____ Get "Thank you" card ready for Tom and set call reminder for 1 week, 1 month and 1 year after close to call

8. _____ Set 7 day reminder for Tom to send birthday card

9. _____ Make sure all checklists are completed, signed off and in files for both pending and listing files

10. _____ Make sure sign and lockbox are down

_____ **Final initials & Date by head broker**

These checklists are used constantly in my office and keep it running smoothly and efficiently beyond most business owners' wildest dreams. For instance, when I take a new listing I give it to my assistant. They then take out a *"New Listing Checklist"* and go through it (see checklist 1a) and for the rest of the business too.

Color Conscious

The next thing to do is color code your files, meaning having different colored file folders for different types of files. Mine are as follows:

-All Red file folders are for listings.

-All Green file folders are for pendings.

-All Yellow file folders are for withdrawn or cancelled listings.

-All Blue file folders are for sale fails.

On the file tab, I put the name, address and phone of the client. Then next to it, I put a sticker representing the year in which it either closed or when we were dealing with it.

Having an office with systems in place is the best and most efficient way to run a great business. Even if you say that you do not own your own business because you work for another broker, you still have to have a great system in place to be profitable and your broker will love you and respect you more. Besides, you really do own your business; you're just not realizing it yet.

A great system frees up your time more to be doing what is most important – and that is listing and selling homes.

Right now my most important thing to do is to go generate leads and look for business in the morning. Then in the afternoon, I return calls, talk to my existing clients, initial paperwork and list homes for sale. Everything else in the business is delegated to someone else that can do a great job.

The acronym KISS is a great motto to live by when it comes to designing your system – keep it simple stupid. That's what you have to keep doing in your business. By keeping it very simple, you relieve the stress of running your business and you make it more enjoyable.

Your Team

A successful business owner is only as good as his or her team members. That is why it is imperative that with your simple system in place, you have a team to back up your system. Your team could include:
-A listing agent
-A buyer's agent
-A transaction coordinator
-A listing coordinator
-A home stager (part-time)

Listing Agent

The listing agent's duties are as follows:
-Looking for homes to sell
-Following up with potential leads
-Going on listing appointments and taking listings
-Negotiating
-Taking care of their sellers with great communication
The listing agent should have the least to do. Here is my perfect day as a listing agent. I show up for work and look for listings two to three hours per day. I go to lunch and then return calls and call my sellers to touch base and ask for price reductions if they are not selling. Then I negotiate offers and after that I do all my listing appointments at a specific time and take listings. Then I do all of my follow-up with potential listings

The New Age Real Estate Agent

before I go home.

The business thrives on new listings; it is the life blood of real estate. It takes way less time to take a listing, price it right, and have it sell then it does to work with buyers. Plus, by having listings, the buyers automatically come anyway. They come from having listings, and good ones.

I never take on anything else in the business because I want to keep my focus on just taking listings, that's all. I never get caught up in the stories that develop with each deal, because I learned a long time ago that every deal has it's own special story; they all do, they all will.

After I negotiate the sale of one of my listings, I tell the seller that my transaction coordinator will soon be in touch to close the deal and that I will still be in touch on a weekly basis. Then, before each call every week, I ask my closing coordinator how that deal is going and then touch base with my seller. If they ask about a certain situation, I then tell them that my closing coordinator will be on it and they will call them with any immediate news.

My sellers are always OK with doing business this way because they respect and trust me. This is the reason why they hired me to list their home. Besides, when I sign the listing contract with them, I tell them exactly what will happen after their home goes under contract – who will be in touch with them and why. They are always alright with it, as long as I tell them up front with no surprises.

I am also studying the market by doorknocking because I am out in the trenches daily and see what is going on. This is huge, because I am at the heartbeat of what the market is doing and, more important, what it will potentially do. So in a listing presentation, I tell the sellers this and they know it too because they see me out there all the time. I walk the walk.

Now, here is the real secret to how I run my office...are you ready? Write this down or bookmark this page immediately.

I run it like a doctor's office. That's right. I run it like a doctor's office!

When the seller comes in for their market analysis or to list their home, the first thing they walk into is a professional office that looks great and has a beautiful atmosphere. They are greeted by the assistant/listing coordinator with a clipboard and form to fill out. The assistant will ask them if they would like any coffee or water and make sure they are comfortable. Then after filling out the form, my assistant takes it back to me in my office where I read it before I greet the client. Then I go out and greet them and take them back to the conference room where there is a big, flat-screen video monitor hooked up to the computer and MLS system.

We both go through the MLS and I show them what the market is doing and show them comparable homes to theirs. This is way more efficient than meeting them at their house with just a few slips of paper and telling them I have done a market analysis for them. Besides, there have been a number of times where I showed up before with the papers to their home and unknowingly not had the correct information. It is more professional and they respect that fact.

It also puts me in control of the situation instead of them being in control. I always tell myself that it is a red flag if they insist on me going to their house, because there is always a reason why. Do they want to sell me on the $50,000 drapes they just put in? Or the beautiful, bright red they just painted the kitchen? Whatever the reason, it's because they want to be in control. You have to realize that when you are at a person's house and they are interviewing you for the job of selling their home, you are not in control, they are! So, by having them come to your office for the listing, it puts you in control of the whole situation.

I have a home stager that I pay to go over and check out the house *after* we put it on the market. After all, why play games? You obviously know the market now that you actually own it. You are living and breathing it on a daily basis now. When someone says they live on such and such a street, then you have a pretty good idea as to what the value of their home is. Why do you need to go see it? I've heard them all and none of them make sense to me. If the house is so special, then just have the seller bring in a list of everything they think is different or that will improve the value of their home. I always tell them that I have to go about it very objectively just like a buyer and buyer's agent does. This is another thing my company does great coaching on and you can read more about this in chapter 10.

Buyer's Agent

The buyer's agent's duties are as follows:
-Looking for new business
-Following up with potential leads
-Showing and selling buyers' homes
-Handling all inspections and appraisals
-Negotiating
-Taking care of the buyers with great communication
-Establishing a great relationship with buyers and working for their needs, ***not the needs of the agent***
Buyer agents should come into the office first thing in the

morning and look for leads, either on the phone or by visiting the buyers they already know are ready to buy a home today. When the business flows really well, a great buyer's agent will get referrals on a daily basis because of the great customer service they always give. But until then, they have to look for business and follow-up when they first get into the office. Then they should have a specific time to work the deals that are currently under contract.

By having a specific time to get any and all jobs done is the best mindset they can have. It takes the stress out of each deal because they know how long it will take and the buyer and other agent know this, too, so there will not be any surprises. Also, when they first come into the office, their energy is best spent on new deals instead of frantically rushing around putting fires out with their pending deals. To make the business fun and exciting, they need to develop this mindset.

So it is a must to set up a schedule where they have a specific time in the afternoon to work on the deals under contract. This even means setting up all the inspections, appraisals and so on in the afternoon. Even when an inspector tells them that the only time to come is in the morning, they should tell them that it does not fit in their schedule and that afternoons are best.

This is also a fine line to running a successful business and being popular with a lot of friends, because when a buyer's agent gets really good, most of the buyers become your best friend and want to spend any extra time that you have with you.

When showing and selling buyers' homes, they need to be very, very efficient in the process. Lizbeth, and I have found it really simple and easy to just e-mail the client MLS printouts of the homes they like and let the buyers drive by and tell us if they are interested in seeing them or not. I remember when I first got

The New Age Real Estate Agent

my license, I drove around buyers until gas ran out of my car, seeing home after home and never really getting anywhere because they always forgot any homes after about three or four, then it was all a big blur. So let the buyers drive themselves around and see which neighborhoods they like and don't like. Then, when they see something they like, e-mail it to them and even have them come into the office to write it up – subject to them approving it! We have done many deals this way and have found that the buyers even like it more because they are not tied down to us and having to spend all day with us chit-chatting about nothing.

We also own our own mortgage company, so most of everything is done in-house, like a one-stop shop. We have the buyers fill out and sign papers disclosing to them that they fully understand that they do not have to go through us for their mortgage and it will not hurt a deal in any way. Once we get that out of the way, we get them pre-approved to see how much they can and want to afford. After seeing what type of payment they want to handle, then we do printouts of some homes they are interested in. By the way, everything is done on a huge, flat-screen video monitor with them so we are all together on the same page. Once we find three or four homes that they like, we do a printout and tell them to go drive by them and let us know what they think.

If they call back with one that they really liked, then we write up an offer subject to their approval of the inside and the inspection report. Now you might be thinking, "How can you write an offer on something you have never seen!?" My reply is always the same, it's easy. It's easy because we have the mindset and we have introduced it to the client also. So since we are the professionals and they are not and they trust and respect us, they

The New Age Real Estate Agent

will do as we suggest without thinking about it. Remember, you get what you attract to yourself.

So by doing business this way, you are not only cutting your time in half if not more, but you are able to focus on more buyers or your family! Don't go to work just to go to work, life is way to short. If you sold three homes this week already and all are going smooth with little care and follow-up, do not feel guilty – look for more business or go home to your family and have a great life. If you don't have a family, go out and have fun then!

This mindset only works when others around you are doing the same and there is a great support system in place with your peers. Otherwise, the ones who do not do business this way will try to pull you down to their level and you will be just like them sooner or later.

When negotiating, the buyer's agent needs to get really good at this and do their best for the buyer. It will all start with the respect that the buyer has for the buyer's agent. If the buyer does not respect them, then it will take a lot longer for the deal to happen. So the respect comes from many different things. It comes from any number of the following: name recognition, the way the agent first sets things up in the beginning, how the agent perceives themselves, the way the agent treats and respects the buyer, and so on. Obviously, the more rapport the buyer's agent has with the buyers, the better and smoother things will go.

When in the middle of a deal, the buyers always try calling at different times of the day and with different emotions. Realize where they are coming from – for instance, if you have a buyer that is being really difficult and needs to know things right now! Put yourself in their mindset for the moment so you can relate to them and do a great job communicating.

To make a smooth process with the buyers, the agent

needs to explain at the beginning how things work. The agent explains that all calls pertaining to the deal are called at a certain time of the day and that the agent's time is best spent ***running*** the business instead of being in a "fire extinguish" mode.

When working with a transaction coordinator, even they have to have a schedule as to when buyers are dealt with, too. But this must be explained in the beginning also.

It just comes to down to great communication and not letting the business run the agent. The agent, the owner and the families are happier in the long run.

Making the needs of the buyer come before the needs of the agent is crucial. You might ask, "How can I do that *and* tell them *when* I can talk and when I can't?" The answer is simple again – tell them up front in the beginning. Also, it should be noted that the more respect and trust they have of the agent, the less worried they will be calling the agent all the time. If you have a client calling you all the time, maybe it's a sign that you need to do a better job for them.

Pertaining to writing up deals, make it best for the buyer, not the agent! I have seen too many agents impose their own beliefs and values onto deals, resulting only in bad feelings and wasted time. Remember that by getting the agent's ego out of the way and actually listening with both ears to what the buyer wants, it will let the buyer get what they really want. The agent can use stories that are similar to theirs when a situation comes up that they need to advise the buyer on. But this can and only should be used if the agent has actually lived through it. Otherwise, it is dishonest and the buyer will see right through that. This is why getting coached by someone who has actually sold homes before is crucial because they can offer advise on the subject and not impose their own beliefs. And if the agent does not know the answer then they can always say, "That's a great question, let me check on that for you."

The law of attraction is perfect here, too. If you are a buyer's agent and want to be more successful with buyers, then they will come by setting up your systems the way it will attract them.

Transaction Coordinator

The transaction coordinator's duties are as follows:
- Filling out all the proper paperwork and checklists
- Calling and keeping in great communication with the clients
- Filing and taking care of the files
- Making sure all transactions are going smoothly
- Making sure all contracts and files have proper signatures and dates
- Making sure agents are paid correctly with commissions

When a deal goes into contract, the first thing the transaction coordinator does is make sure they fill out and use the first checklist. Then they make a file and color code it. Their job is to be in control of all the color-coded files and the system you have set up. The office runs much smoother this way, especially when someone has a question on a particular file and the transaction coordinator is not around to ask. Then they can go right into the file and even look at the notes to see where everyone is at with the deal. It also keeps everything in perfect order for auditing purposes or management.

Calling and keeping in great communication with the

clients and all pertaining parties is of huge value to the business and is one of the transaction coordinator's main duties. The real estate agent also has to keep in contact on a weekly basis, but the transaction coordinator is more detailed in the knowing. It also is very professional to know that there is one particular person handling the deal and that there are detailed notes on the file.

The client usually wants to be in the know of what is happening and this way there is one person who is in great communication with them.

Filing and taking care of the files is a major factor in running a successful business. We have been visited by the state before and every time they come, they always leave with the same remark, "It is a pleasure to come here and see the way you keep your files. They are in order and very clean. We are impressed!" So when a deal starts to go bad and things do not end up the way you thought, you have complete records with notes. You get to go back in time and see who did what and when, whose responsibility was whose and why, etc...

It is the job of the transaction coordinator to make sure the deals are going smoothly. They control the files, the notes and everything that pertains to the deal and they are in charge of a smooth closing.

The transaction coordinator has more of a lenient schedule in that they are in more of the "putting out fire" mode, but must not be looked upon this way. The closer they can get to running a tighter schedule, the better off and more productive they are. They must be full of energy and express that to all they come into contact with. Could you imagine talking with one that sounds like a beat-up telemarketer? No, they have to be brave and answer everyone's questions by staying in control and being very detailed at the same time.

The New Age Real Estate Agent

They also have to make sure all contracts and files have proper signatures and dates at all times by being in total control of the files and notes. There are laws in each state that require the broker/owner to read and initial all documents within a certain period of time. Ultimately, it is the job of the broker/owner to make sure everything is initialed and dated where and when it is supposed to be, but working together with the transaction coordinator will make sure a clean and perfect system is in place and working.

And, last but not least, they need to make sure all the agents are paid the full commissions due to them and on time. This is done with complete and detailed follow up on each and every transaction. I have seen a number of times where the title company or a lawyer has not calculated the bottom line correctly and still a property was closed. This is an unprofitable and careless way to run a company.

The checklists to use go through this and should be double-checked on each closing, if not triple-checked, with the agent involved, too. You work hard for your commissions and so this area deserves extra attention.

Listing Coordinator

The listing coordinator's duties are as follows:
- Answer all incoming calls and set listing appointments, plus screen all incoming calls
- Enter all new listings into MLS system
- Do all price changes, withdrawals, expireds and any listing changes
- Take all photos of new listings

The New Age Real Estate Agent

- Enter all data into Web sites and any changes (including photos)
- Deliver pre-list packs
- Make flyers for listings
- Make flyers for door-knocking
- Schedule personal appointments for owner
- Remind all agents of upcoming appointments
- Call all sellers with feedback on all listings
- E-mail or mail weekly sellers' report
- Keep track of conference room schedule
- Keep track of listing agent's schedule
- Keep track of weekly office meetings
- Keep track of inventory and order supplies
- Keep listing agent on tight schedule

The listing coordinator has a lot of small things to do and keep track of. This person has to be very bright, full of energy, have a sense of humor, be on time and be assertive. I have been through many assistants and the ones that work have been the ones that I described above.

I have always fired the ones that have a habit of coming in five minutes late everyday. If the office opens its doors at 9 a.m., that means the assistant comes in at 8:50 a.m. and is ready to go at 9 a.m.

I can read a lot about a person if they are always late in life. It shows disrespect to others and the focus is usually about them. They usually always have an excuse as to why they are late and never even try to get in the habit of being somewhere on time. When an assistant shows up even five minutes late on a continual basis and the phones have been ringing for five minutes, this is unacceptable because the client also expects the office to be open when they say it will be open.

The New Age Real Estate Agent

The listing coordinator answers all incoming calls with a smile on their face and full of energy. They answer with a great greeting like, "It's a wonderful day at The Hale Group and Lendingman Mortgage. How may I help you?" Or if you are working for another broker, as soon as the call is patched through to your assistant ,you can have a similar greeting. So if you have an office within an office, make sure you call your team a name like, "The John Smith Group" and have your assistant answer the phone, "It's another powerful day at the John Smith Group. How may I help you?"

The listing coordinator sets up all listing appointments to come into the office. They use a script and role play it with the listing agent or owner everyday of the week for five minutes before starting to answer calls. They are in charge of pre-qualifying all the appointments, too. The listing coordinator must screen all calls that come through so as not to waste anyone's time. When someone calls in and they just ask for me, then it is their job to ask them to what it pertains. Usually, the listing coordinator can handle the questions that are asked, but if they cannot then they will take a message for whoever it is for. In the end, they must be looked upon as the guard at the gate of the castle – nothing gets through, no matter what. There are a lot of advertising firms or people that want to sell the owner something and waste their time and some of these people are very sneaky at doing so.

Once a new listing comes in, the listing agent gives them the contract and they start to use the "New Listing Checklist." Then, when they are finished with it, they give it back for the listing agent's final initials. The listing coordinator is in charge of all price changes, withdrawals, expireds and any changes to the listing itself.

The New Age Real Estate Agent

After any changes are done, they give a copy to the listing agent to initial for final approval. That way in case there was an error, it goes to the responsibility of the licensed listing agent.

They are in charge of taking great photos of each listing and entering them on the MLS system and all Web sites. They are trained to take great looking photos that will attract buyers and agents, too.

After an appointment has been set for a listing, then they immediately hand-deliver a pre-list pack with a note to the door of the seller. This includes all current sales by the agent and a note saying that the agent looks forward to meeting them at a certain time.

They are in charge of making all flyers for each listing (we do not use them, but instead use an 800 callback system). They are also in charge of making all door-knocking flyers and having them ready at least three days in advance for the agent to deliver.

Another responsibility they have is to schedule all personal appointments for either the owner or the listing agent. This is agreed upon when they are first hired. There are plenty of times when I needed to either see a dentist, doctor, lawyer or even get my haircut. This is a very big issue because the job of the assistant is to keep the agent on schedule and not on the phone. They also have on file all credit cards, hotel rewards info., families phone numbers and so on. They also remind the agent of all upcoming events and appointments. They must be looked at upon as an extension of the listing agent.

They are in charge of calling and being in direct communication with all sellers for feedback on showings. They also e-mail or mail the sellers with a weekly report on their listing and even set up any tours or open houses with the seller.

The New Age Real Estate Agent

Additionally, they keep track of conference room schedules, the listing agent's schedule and the buyer's agent schedule, too. They are also in charge of keeping track of all inventory for office supplies and have a checklist for that, too. It is imperative that the office never has to shut down because the toner ran out or there is no paper to print out a contract with a client ready to sign. The inventory checklist must be done on a weekly basis and given to the owner for them to initial.

Most importantly, the listing coordinator must keep the listing agent on their schedule at all costs. Because taking listings and a lot of them is the number one job for the listing agent. The more the listing agent can be in front of willing and able sellers, the better off the whole business runs...period. The listing coordinator has many job titles and this must be explained when they are hired in the beginning. I have even had someone not do something pertaining to the job and tell me that it was not in their job description when they were hired. So make sure everything is up front and that they are willing to do what it takes to make and run a successful, profitable company.

Home Stager

The part-time home stager's duties are as follows:

-Set all home-staging appointments and keep track of their own schedule

-Keep track of all completed home-staged properties

-Bill listing agent for all completed home-staged properties

-Call and set all appointments with any contractors, painters, etc., that need to do work on property

The New Age Real Estate Agent

When a listing is first taken, it is agreed upon by the listing agent and the seller that the home will be staged. Staged meaning that the home stager goes through the whole house with a checklist room by room – checking off what furniture needs to go where, what walls need to be painted or repainted, what carpets need replacing and so on. It is the job of the home stager to go through the house and tell the seller what to do before putting it on the market, instead of the listing agent.

The home stager must be a licensed home stager and be familiar with interior design. We have always had our transaction coordinator in charge of this and run as their separate business. I, as the listing agent, hire them every time I take a new listing and they are paid no matter if the house sells or not. They are doing a professional job and need to get paid for their services immediately. This, in turn, makes me price the home at true market value even better, because I am not profitable if it does not sell because I paid the home stager for their services.

They are in charge of keeping track of calling and setting up all appointments with the fresh, new listings and keeping track of all completed ones, too.

They are in charge of calling the sellers with all contractors (by giving them a choice of at least three) and maybe setting up the appointments if the sellers are not home or living in property.

They are in charge of billing the listing agent for all completed home-staged properties and run a business within a business. By having a home stager, it not only makes you look more professional, but things run smoother, too. I always tell my sellers that it is my job to sell their home, not be an interior decorator. I also tell them that their house will sell faster for more amount of money because when it goes on the market, we want the house to show very well like a model home does.

That is the whole team! Using such a team, and a series of easy checklists to plan your work, it's a very simple system that you can do hundreds of deals with. Some of the other benefits include:

-Small team with *huge* profits

-Everyone knows their position and what is expected of them, so there is less stress in the office atmosphere

-The listing agent can work minimal hours and spend more time with family, hobbies, or? (I usually work only 125 days per year while owning and running other businesses, such as TR HALE Real Estate coaching)

-The system is clean and simple

So start today, put these systems in place immediately, and you will see fast results. Start out by implementing a few per week so you can still focus on your job and what you have to do. When there is turnover in your business or when someone is sick, just refer to using the checklists and most of your stress will be alleviated.

The New Age Real Estate Agent

Chapter 6

Making a Popular Logo and Branding Yourself

"The price of greatness is responsibility."
Winston Churchill

The New Age Real Estate Agent

Making a popular logo is a key point and one that will separate you from the rest. By having a logo that gets recognized by most people in your area will give you name recognition and at the same time develop trust
in the community about who you are and what you stand for.

It also keeps you in the front mind of everyone, where you want to be. When someone in your community has the need to sell, whether it be for divorce, job transfer, moving up, or down, etc…you need to be the first agent that comes to their mind. When you think of a drink, do you think of Coca Cola? Or do you think of another one? My point is, you think of the one that is the easiest, the most simple to remember, and has marketed the heck out of your brain to remember them. Coke comes to mind when I am on the road and go into a convenient store to quench my thirst. Now, that being said, I don't want you to go out and capture a market and provide lousy service. Because you still can, but it is not only unethical, but you will never grow your business to the fullest potential that you could have in the first place, and, of course, it will cost you in the long run.

So what is a popular logo? It is something that is easy for everyone to remember, it needs to be simple, fun and friendly, and that's all. It needs to eventually stand for you selling their home or helping find one for them. It also stands for the plain and simple fact that you are the real estate expert in their area.

My first business that I started and owned was my windsurfing industry. I knew that I needed a logo to put on the sails that would be visible on the water and even on land, so people could see it no matter what (see chapter 2). So I came up with this character that I even gave a name to, Mast Head Roy.

The New Age Real Estate Agent

He was very simple, fun and friendly! I even sold him as a sticker so people could put them on their cars, sails or whatever. I made him huge so he could be seen everywhere, especially if you had him on your sail far from land. I marketed him in the local newspapers with his own ad that ran weekly. He used to have a megaphone coming out of his mouth and say a new weekly saying like, "Mast Head Roy says, "Shaka dude!" or, "Shred till you're dead!" This was put in the local papers and people could not get enough of it. They would stop me on the beach and ask, "Hey, what does Mast Head Roy say today?"

Again, keeping even the advertising simple because there is usually so much to read in a newspaper that people just want to get through it fast. When people saw Mast Head Roy, they thought of my windsurfing business. That's all. They thought of something that was fun and cool. They wanted to be a part of it because everyone else was a part of it.

Mast Head Roy

The New Age Real Estate Agent

So, by taking the time to brainstorm and come up with a catchy logo will definitely pay off. Some helpful hints are to remember that you need to match the logo with what you are and who you stand for. For instance, if you sell the upper-end homes (which I highly suggest you do), then come up with a classy logo – one that represents style, class and expensive taste. But be careful not to overdo it to the point that it is hard for everyone to remember. On another side, be careful not to make it tacky with pictures of you and animals together, unless of course you sell farms and ranches. Get it? Great! Easy enough.

Now, if you work for a company and the owner/ manager has his logo on for sale signs and you can only put your name on, then consider this – ask them if you can make your own logo next to your picture on all the future ads that you do, including the for sale signs and directional signs. You still will have their company and you can put your own picture next to your logo. Be careful not to correlate both of them together, however. You want people to remember you, and your broker should be happy because you are promoting them, too.

Now this is what my wife and I did. We both went to a professional photographer and had our photos shot together. On some of the photos, we were standing hand in hand, some with our backs to each other, but looking very professional and some really friendly. So when choosing, we thought what would be the best way to brand ourselves in our market and have people remember us?

We ended up choosing one where we were standing (a full-length shot) with our backs to each other and arms crossed with big smiles looking forward. This, we thought, looked very professional, friendly and inviting. Then we contracted out to someone that made a logo in the background. This logo was of our area mountain in the background and our names, "The Hales." After making that, we put that on every printed form of advertising we could find. Our job was to get market awareness from the people in our local area and it worked! This is a long-term way to look at it.

There are so many agents out there that want success right now and, by God, if they don't get it in the first six months, then to hell with it all! Do you think McDonald's or any other successful company started out with this mindset?

Remember, this is long term that you are doing this, and to make a career out of it. Does it take that long for the name recognition to happen? No. In our case, it took about one year, but the results kept getting better after three years. For example, we (my wife and I) had already been in the real estate business selling homes for about eight years before we started this new way of selling. We were making a moderate income of about $200,000 a year. But the way we got the business was from cold-calling expireds. We also got a lot of FSBOs listed and sold them, too. We were selling a whole metropolitan area of homes and not focusing on one particular area.

When we started this new way of doing business and owning an area, though, I knew that our first year would be a slight drop in income. It was because I was no longer on that treadmill of being at the market's whim – expireds and FSBOs – and I was trying to focus on a smaller area (but more powerful). We had it in our business plan that we would only make an income of about $150,000 to $175,000. Again, this would be due to looking for leads in a different way and totally changing our business around. Guess what? It came true! That first year, we only did about $168,000 for the year. But I had kept track of all the numbers, especially the actual contacts per listing. It was around the ratio of 150 contacts to a listing. So I knew that I just had to go out and make more contacts in my area to do more business. While, at the same time, I was marketing us (my wife and I) and name branding us in our area! After all, you don't get something for nothing.

Finding Your Brand/Logo

Branding is done by nearly every successful business in the world. For instance, how many times do you see all these real estate ads with all these pictures of the agents running the ad? Do you actually remember that particular agent? Chances are that you do not. But if that agent just did something a little different and had a logo next to them <u>and</u> consistently ran that ad and logo together, then the image would slowly burn into your mind. Now, does it matter if that agent was the top 1% or the worst producer in history? No! Of course, if they want more business coming back to them as mentioned earlier, then they would provide great customer service after they get the business so they can stay in business.

As far as names are concerned and you want your name to be the brand, then I hope it is a small and simple name. I have that advantage because "Hale" is easy to remember, just like "Trump" or "Coke." But my point is, KISS – keep it simple, stupid! Make your logo not only simple but powerful and one that people will remember no matter what. If it's not the name you are branding, then design a simple, fun logo or hire someone to do this for you. And most importantly, just stick to it and keep using it and using it. Believe me – you will get sick of your own logo before anyone else does.

After you have established one, then use it on everything – fax cover sheets, car signs, bus benches, flyers, magnets, everything and anything you put out there with your name on it. I have seen a lot of agents copy me and the way I do business. But it is funny how I never get a call from any one of these people. I would probably share with them how to do things (or my impression of) if they only asked. It's not such a secret; the only secrets are the ones they actually think I can't hear. If they only did things on a consistent basis and hung out with others that supported them, or better yet, had the courage to stand alone for what they believed and had faith.

The New Age Real Estate Agent

Chapter 7

Advertising

"Each time someone stands up for an ideal, or acts to improve the lot of others, or strikes out against injustice, he sends forth a tiny ripple of hope."

Robert F. Kennedy

When I say advertising, what do you think of? Do you think of money flying out of your pocket and into thin air? Do you think of sometimes running a small ad one or two times in your local real estate magazine? Or do you think of something that is for the people that can afford it?

These are all wrong ways to think about advertising. In the first place, let's not call it advertising, OK? Let's call it, "branding," or better yet, let's call it, "reminding people of what you do." OK, now we have that out of the way.

The New Age Real Estate Agent

Direct Response and Institutional Ads

The next thing to think about is the big buzz of *"Direct Response"* or *"Institutional"* advertising. What are they and what's the difference?

Direct response basically means that you run an ad and expect to get immediate results. It tells the consumer why, how or where to buy something and a call to action to do a certain thing now. They say that direct response is the only way to track how you are spending your advertising dollars since you can count the calls coming in and tie them to a particular ad. Great, you say! Yes, it works for the fast buck but does not create loyalty with the consumer. It is a very cheesy way to do business, in my opinion. The companies that promote it say that it is a far better way to do business because you can track where your dollars are going. Do you really have time to do that?

Here would be a good example of using direct response advertising: a real estate agent puts an ad in the local paper that says, "I am the neighborhood expert. Call me for your free market analysis now at #######!" "Call me now for your free market update!" or "Would you like to see how much your home has increased in value in the past six months?" "Call me now at ######!" or "I just sold this beautiful home on SE 124th St. Call me today at ###### to find out how much yours is worth!"

These were all done with the following on each ad:
- Full color glossy
- A catch to have the consumer be interested enough to read
- A call to action to do something now!
- Lots of white space for the eye to only focus on what

you want them to do

Do any of these sound familiar to you? Well, they do to me, because these are some of mine that I did for years and they hardly paid for themselves.

Direct response advertising is great for things like selling a bike on the Web, looking to hire an assistant to help you out in the business, putting a flyer out for your lost dog, etc... Does that make sense? Don't get me wrong, but direct response has no place in real estate sales unless you really need a fast response for an open house or something of that nature, or you just want to get buyers to call you. But if you ever want to make the big bucks in real estate, you will spend most of your time advertising to sellers like I do.

They also say that you will spend less money on direct response adverting. No, you won't! Yes, if you work like an average agent out there who is looking for the quick buck. I hope you are better than that and want to build a long and extremely profitable business.

By doing fewer ads, yes, you will spend less but will you be *known* in your area that you are capturing? No. You will be just another agent with their high school photo in hopes that someone will respond to your one listing so you can make a fast sell!

Research says that the public will send more money when they know more about the product. The product is you!

Now let's talk about *institutional* or corporate advertising. The definition is advertising for an organization rather than its products. The purpose is to build a positive image in the eyes of the public. It does not attempt to sell anything directly. It is also called corporate advertising.

The New Age Real Estate Agent

With institution advertising, it works on a lower conscious level. You are constantly in the public's eye. The public is not really aware that they are gaining a positive impression, but they are because they associate you with your product in the area and that you have high professionalism.

The positive aspects of institutional advertising far outweigh the direct response way, especially when you are taking over a target area in real estate. Why?

Because:.

-You build rapport with the public as being the market leader in the area. (It appears to be even if you are not).

- You build trust with the public because they see you have been around for a while and you will be first on their minds when selling or buying a home.

- You have people calling you on a consistent basis to come list their home. I have had many people call me and say, "Tom. we want to sell our home and have always known that we would call you when the time was right. We have seen your name all over and knew you were the area expert!"

- You do not need to cold call and waste your time and or the public's time.

- You do not need to call the bottom of the barrel expireds (as I call them) and try to win over someone who does not trust you in the first place.

So here is how to implement institutional advertising with real estate. Last year, I only spent 3% of my total income on advertising (institutional). Two to three hours a day in the morning was spent on doorknocking on my segway. Now, you can look for leads any other way. I just found that being face-to-face with people in my target area is the best for me, because I

The New Age Real Estate Agent

get to know them and they trust me through always seeing my bus benches, flyers and other things that I do. Being on a segway (see one at www.segway.com), I am able to hit 150 to 200 doors a day and then go back to the office with a lot of energy, as opposed to only being able to doorknock 80 to 100 on foot and go home for a nap afterwards. Not to mention, walking takes twice the time, too, and is not as much fun.

Oh yes, people everyday try to give me a bad time because I am not getting my exercise. I tell them that I get up at 5 a.m. and either swim, bike or run for a straight hour. That usually quiets them down. Besides, when they see a person on a strange thing like a segway wearing a big smile coming down the street, usually they do not know how to act. But the ones that know me now think that it is the coolest thing to be doing! Even the ones that don't know me will stop and ask, "Is that thing fun?" or "How do you keep your balance on that thing?" So it's a real ice breaker and most people automatically respect me because I have the courage to do what I want to and not be average. This is how I like to see it.

Just the other day, it was time to send out the monthly mailers to our target area. My wife said to me that we really needed to save that money this month because we just closed on another big property for ourselves and needed the cash flow. Advertising, or "reminding people what you do," is essentially just that. You need to keep in front of the public eye so that you are first on their minds when they are in need of you. So I had to convince my wife again of the importance of consistently doing this (institutional advertising). You need to be the first one on the consumer's mind when they are thinking of real estate and consistently keeping your name in front of them will only make things better.

The New Age Real Estate Agent

One way to look at it is to think about every time your sellers want you to run an ad in your local real estate magazine for their home. Are you to do direct response or institutional advertising?

A lot of sellers want direct response because there are agents out there that really try to sell this to their sellers. The agents tell them that they will do this and the sellers will have a lot of calls coming in on the ad. Yes, the phone might ring, but it will be from someone that has more questions about the property and if the agent is up on their skills, they will convert them to another home because chances are they will not be interested in the house they call in on.

So why not really understand how this works and then tell the truth to your sellers. Say something like this, "Mr. and Mrs. Seller, the reason I run ads in the local real estate magazine is to promote myself and my company and to make the phone ring with new buyers. I will be switching your home ad with all the other homes that I have listed on a monthly basis. You have to understand that the real reason I do this is to basically make the phone ring for my business and to keep my name in front of people at all times, does that make sense? You did say that the reason you wanted me to sell your home is because you have seen us everywhere, right? Well, this is the way I do my business and thank you for understanding."

Telling your sellers the truth and having integrity with yourself to keep doing that is by far the best thing to do. Your clients will respect you and you will respect yourself, therefore building more confidence each and every day.

I have always shuddered at the client that wants to advertise here and do open houses there. This type of person is very demanding and tries to be in control of you and the situation. It took me a long time to finally stand up to these people (in a nice way) and just tell them that I am the wrong person to sell their home.

The reason why I do not like or do open houses is because they are very unproductive for the seller. Mostly is all you get are the nosey neighbors that want to see the home so they can find out how much their own home will sell for. Or they are just curious and have nothing better to do so they walk next door and waist the agents time.

Now on the other hand, I have seen them be very productive with agents that do them all the time and get a lot of business this way (mostly buyers). The agent will advertise everywhere that they do open houses and really talk it up that they do business this way. A lot of sellers buy into this way of selling homes and think that this is the way to bring offers in. But my opinion is opposite because I would rather tell the seller the truth about how they work.

Sometimes I get a seller that tells me, "We bought our home through an open house" and my response is usually, "Great, you were one of the 5% nationwide that actually made an offer through an open house!" Then I say, "Mr and Mrs Seller, I would rather actively promote your property instead of passively wait for someone to walk in and upon happenstance, purchase your property....does that make sense"?

Open houses are great for the new agent or buyers agent (agent that works only with buyers) that wants more buyers. But if you want to own your target area you will want to deal mostly with sellers and have someone else on your team do the open houses so they can get buyers to buy your other listings. Remember, you will have a lot of new listings in your target area that you can show buyers to. Not just one listing in one particular area and not give the buyer a choice.

So again, use institutional advertising as a way of branding yourself and keeping in the publics eye. They will remember who you are and when it comes time to sell or buy, they will think of you first.
This is key and must be done.
If you do not do any self promotion and believe that people will know who you are just because......because of what?!!! It will not work this way and there are plenty of big egos in this business like that.
If you do not want your picture then make a memorable logo or vise versa, just get something out there and keep it out there!

Chapter 8

Numbers, Numbers, Numbers

"The function of leadership is to produce more leaders, not more followers."

Ralph Nader

I used to cold call for years and did not enjoy it all until I finally took responsibility for my outcome. At first, it was sitting at my desk going through the phone book and calling all the people in my area to see if they wanted to buy or sell a home. I would actually make a checkmark for every person I dialed. Here is the very first script that I used:

Hello, my name is Tom Hale with _____ and I was calling to see if you planned on selling your home now or in the near future."

The New Age Real Estate Agent

My ratios for the whole year were as follows:
1. Total hours on phone generating leads: 100
2. Total decision makers talked to: 1,200
3. Total listing appointments: 10
4. Total listings taken: 5
5. Total listings sold: 3
6. Total buyer appointments: 25
7. Total buyers bought a home: 8
8. Total closed: 11
9. Total days worked: 256\

Any good coaching company out there, whether it be a real estate coaching company or business coaching company, will make you keep track of similar numbers. These numbers are very important to keep track of. Whether you can read these numbers or not, just focus on the total closed I did back then – a scary 11 deals in one year! I think that is more than the average agent sells per year right now, which is even scarier!

So let's go through the numbers together to see what happened. You have heard it said before, "Life is a numbers game."

My plan (in my head) was to work full time at 40 hours a week. It ended up being more like seven days a week and 10 hours a day with 250 days worked for the year. Luckily, I was single at that time. Otherwise, it would have led to an ugly divorce.

In sum, I only prospected for new business 4/10 of an hour per day. I get that by dividing 100 total hours into 256 days worked.

The next number to look at is total decision makers talked to. This means actually talking to them and asking them about real estate. This number was only 1,200 out of 100 hours, which means about 12 contacts per hour. Take 1,200 and divide by 100 and it equals 12 people talked to per hour.

The next number to look at is total listing appointments. This means sitting down or on the phone (more about this later) with both decision makers and presenting to them a plan and a contract to list their home.

The next number to look at is total listings taken. This means a signed contract where they hired you to sell their home. Mine at that time was 50%. Take 10 listing appointments and divide it by five listings taken and you get 50%.

The next number to look at is listings sold ratio. You need to see how good you are at not only taking listings, but getting them sold, too. My number was five listings taken divided by three listings sold, which equals about 60%.

The next number to look at is total buyer sales. Mine was 25 buyers that I worked with (not counting how many homes I showed them each) and eight total homes that I sold them, which equals 32% – not a good number to be proud of.

So the *end result of that year* was to add three total listings sold to total of eight buyer sales, equaling 11 closed and paid transactions. These are pretty typical of an average agent out there right now and even on the high side. But let's really look at this together and diagnose it even further.

It looked like I was good at getting to the office because of the number of days worked. There are a total of 220 working days a year in a typical work calendar year and I was working 256 of them. So my drive was there to achieve my goals. But how many of you really want to live your life to the fullest? Do

The New Age Real Estate Agent

you want to be working (or showing up at the office) and not have any other life? Hmmm…maybe with the divorce rate at 50%, does it mean that you are all real estate agents?

Come on, what a joke to say that you work your butt off in life, and have nothing to show for it. There is way more to life than selling homes! Quit playing small. Haven't you ever wanted to learn the piano? Or wanted to learn how to fly an airplane? Or write a book? Or oil paint or whatever?

Why we are put on this earth, I am not sure of. But I do know this – that while I am here and alive, I want to learn how to do it **all**. That might mean learning how to be a brain surgeon at the ripe age of 88 or going to South Africa to help people dying of AIDS next year. There is so much life to live and it really breaks my heart daily to see everyone stuck where they are at in life. Everyone has a drive. Everyone accomplishes things. But then they get stuck and live on past experiences. Of course, everyone has a great excuse of why they are stuck in life. But ultimately, it is because of their beliefs that they are stuck where they are. So what beliefs are holding you back?

Even most of the top producers are stuck as far as I am concerned. Because they can only focus on one thing at a time and that is real estate and, by God, nothing else!

So, great, you are good at real estate, but what about being the best human being you can be. "But where is the glory in that?" they might ask. "Where are my trophies, my awards, my, my, my…It's all about me!"

Then I say great, go for the awards and telling people how great you are, but live it, experience it, and move on to help other people now – today! I can say this because I myself was once there, too. It was all about me and how many awards and recognition I could get. Hey! It is human nature to want acceptance and recognition, but do it by helping more people than just yourself; learn to think bigger.

Jim Rohn says it best, "Work harder on yourself than you do on your job." And as Zig Ziglar says, "You will get everything you want in life if you just help enough people get what they want in life."

But back to diagnosing myself and my numbers for that year. How we will do this now is just to look at the numbers only and make good, educated assessments of what happened. I will act as if these are not mine and someone else's. Because, in truth, this is how you can get smarter about your business.

So we already talked about days worked for the year and the next to talk about is the number of people I talked to per hour – 12. Not bad, but it could have been better or more efficient. I know of people using double and triple headsets making their contacts (actually talking to a decision maker) at 24 to 36 an hour. I did get into using a double headset and the people that I contacted per hour greatly improved, but my quality of leads fell through because I was just focusing on dialing as fast as I could.

So that's when I thought it would be better to actually see these people face-to-face by door knocking. It was so much more effective that way because I really learned how to use my body as a good communicator and not just my voice and a prayer. I was able to start reading people better and seeing their reaction to certain questions, so I, in turn, was working harder on myself because I wanted to be the best communicator out there and help as many people sell their home as I could. I looked at it as seeing

The New Age Real Estate Agent

that these people needed a great agent – an agent that knew what their market was doing, which was obviously more than them and to help them with what I know and how to price their home correctly and how to sell it for the highest possible price.

So don't get hung up on that number too much. Just know that you need to contact as many people as you can in a day and be very efficient at it. Better yet, don't waste other people's time out there. You only give yourself and other real estate agents a bad name.

Back to the numbers – it looked like my listing appointments were low, especially compared to the amount of days worked! Only 10 appointments in 256 days worked?! Good thing I wasn't married at the time, because my wife would have looked at that and said to me, "What were you doing at the office all that time? Oh, that's right, honey, you were spending your time with that blonde showing her those 50 properties."

So how could I have improved on that? Well, I could have gotten better at my scripts which in turn leads to more appointments. I could have a plan to take so many listings a month. I could have focused on taking more listings than being with buyers (even if they were cute). I could have spent more then 4/10 of an hour on the phone per day. Like say bump it up to 3-4 hours. Hey, what else do you have to do? I know, learn how to play piano! I could have had a schedule. Or better yet, I could have hired a great coach to help me, one that actually sells homes and has put in their own sweat equity in the business!

The New Age Real Estate Agent

The next thing to think about is taking only five listings to the 10 appointments I was on. It showed me that I was only taking them 50% of the time. I must not have been pre-qualifying them. I must not have been talking to the right people. I must have not had a good presentation and lousy skills. Was my heart into it? Yes, big time, but I thought I could do it on my own without guidance.

The listings sold ratio was 3/5 or 60%, which meant that 60% of my listings were selling. This is about the lowest you want that ratio to be. At one time in my career, I remember having 34 active listings all at the same time. This was not good at all, because these people hired me to sell their homes and all I could do was to call them weekly and give excuses as to why their home was not selling. It wasn't until I learned my lesson the hard way to take listings at the right price or really tell the sellers the truth about how to price their home correctly. If I would have focused more on the price at the listing presentation and not on how great I or my company was, then I would have priced them better and received more respect from the sellers for telling them the truth on how real estate is actually sold.

It's not how long your market time is in your particular area. Look at it this way. If you live in a market where the average agent sells a home in 180 days and everyone says that the market is slow and you can see that it is slow, then ask yourself what is going on. Why is it slow? Do people just not want to live there? If they don't, then the prices have to come down to make deals for people or at least have them want to buy there for the good deals. If you live in a market right now where the market is days or hours, what is happening to the prices? They are going straight up, right? So the prices will go up and as soon as buyers and investors feel like they are not getting a good deal anymore, then the market shuts off or slows down.   All of this is real easy if you just take the time and think about what is going on in your market and where it is heading.

My total buyer appointments was eight signed contracts to 25 buyers. That did not include showing those 25 buyers all those homes. What a waste of time! If only I would have focused that energy on taking more quality listings and getting them sold. Instead, too much time was spent working with buyers and not enough on sellers.

I had 11 closed deals total for the year; for some of you, that might be OK, but not for me, not for the return on myself that I invested. I did not want to play small and wanted to do way more than that. Which brings me to a more recent year in my business. Let's look at my new numbers and diagnose them as well: 1. Total hours generating leads: 300

2. Total decision makers talked to: 4,000

3. Total listing appointments: 88

4. Total listings taken: 80

5. Total listings sold: 65

6. Total buyers appointments: 2

7. Total buyers bought home: 2

(My wife acted as part-time buyer's agent and sold 22 homes)

8. Total Closed: 87

9. Total days worked: only 125

The New Age Real Estate Agent

Let's diagnose these numbers and see how I did lately. It looks as if I worked on generating leads a lot more. Take total hours (300) and divide by days worked (125), to equal 2.4 hours a day generating leads.

How many of you came from a job that you had to spend eight productive hours at per day? I used to work in warehouses lifting heavy objects all day long loading and unloading trucks. There was work to be done and I had to spend a full eight hours a day and some weekends at the job giving it my all.

If I look at it that way and compare 2.8 hours of a little unpleasantness compared to eight hours of unpleasantness, I would take the 2.8 hours any day and even add to that number it if I wanted to.

I spoke to 4,000 decision makers. This means that every hour, I spoke to 13.3 decision makers. Since I was door knocking, this number is not bad. It is good because I used a segway, which got me around a lot faster on the pavement. Some of you might want to get into double or triple headset dialing if you are using the phone. But keep in mind that the quality of people that you talk to will go down because you will be focusing more on the contacts instead of the appointments. Still, I feel 13 people per hour is pretty good, so I don't want to focus on getting better at that number if I am door knocking unless I put a hemi on my segway and feed it alcohol for fuel.

My total listing appointments was 88. This means that for only working 125 days, I had 88 people come into my office for a listing presentation, which equaled every 1.4 days. If you are shocked by this number, let me tell you I would be, too, if I really did not understand how it worked out. By capturing a market and

The New Age Real Estate Agent

with everyone knowing who I was, I was getting all the business in the area. How hard it used to be by going on all those expired and FSBO listing presentations, trying to first prove who I was and how I ran my business. And how degrading it was to first walk into a home and have the people automatically look me up and down like I was a used car salesman.

This time, people came into <u>my</u> office and I did not have to prove myself to them because they essentially knew who I was – either through my marketing or by seeing me and shaking my hand at the door!

Out of those 88 I presented to, 80 people decided to sell their homes. This is a ratio of 91%! For every time someone came into my office, there was a 91% chance that I would have a signed listing contract. If you would have asked me 12 years ago if I could ever get that number up to that, I would have said that it was impossible.

Here is how I did that big number. Again, it is in the marketing, the word of mouth of who I was and the overall exposure. It was not because I was lucky, or I was good looking or I was a born salesman or whatever else you want to think. It was because of the time and energy I put into marketing myself and using good sales skills to convert people to make a qualified decision. Of course, I had to learn on my own how to talk to and read people and I got this from my daily activities in the business. So it did take time.

These people were already sold on me before they even came into my office. And when they did come in, it was I who was in control because I ran it like a doctor's office. They came in and the first thing that happened was they were greeted by my assistant at the door with a questionnaire to fill out. Then, after they were done with that, my assistant would give it to me in my office. Then I would come out and greet them and take them back to our conference room to begin a quick, short meeting to list their home.

So, for the person that reads this and wants to go from zero to 100 deals in six months, it's not going to happen unless you get lucky. The universe will not reward you, you have not deserved it yet. Remember, the lottery winner that won the $356 million and lost it all, ending up in debt? He did not deserve it.

Now, the listing taken to listing sold ratio is 81%. This means that for every listing I took, there was an 81% chance that it would sell. How did this number also increase? Because I focused more on motivated people that wanted to sell and not just put their home on the market in hopes it would sell at their price, not the market price. I did this by pre-qualifying them better before I had them come into the office. I did this by talking mainly on the price of their home, instead of how great I or my company was.

When people take the time to interview a real estate agent or hire anyone to help them professionally, they don't want to hear about anything else but the truth, what and why it will happen.

Here is a great example. I just had two landscapers come to my house while I was writing this book. I told them what I wanted and how often I wanted it. They both gave me two different bids. It does not matter which bid I chose. It matters that they did not waste my time in telling me what they think I wanted to hear. The landscaper I chose did not waste my time telling me anything else. I already knew and believed he could do the job, because his business promotes all over my area and one was a referral, so it was a really quick process to tell me what I wanted to hear and that was how much and how often.

Focus on that with your clients. Sit them down at your office and ask them what they want. Chances are, it will be:

- How much will my property go for?
- How long will it take?

Pretty simple, huh? And if it's anything else they want, then tell them the truth and don't waste their or your time.

My total buyer appointments and solds was only two! This is because I ran my business the way I wanted to run it and not work with buyers. My wife wanted to deal with them, so she sold them the homes. But let me tell you how she did it. She saw how I was listing all of my homes without ever seeing them in the first place, so she applied it to buyers. She would get a buyer and pre-qualify them to make sure they were motivated and willing to buy a home as soon as she found them something. Then she would tell them how she worked. She told them that they would need to get pre-approved through our lending company that we owned or to get pre-approved with another reputable lending institution. Then she told them that she would e-mail them some properties that they had to drive around and see. They would let her know which ones they liked or did not like based on the looks of the house and neighborhood. By doing this, she really cut her time in half when dealing with buyers. She did not have the expense of driving them around, listening to their personal stories or whatever. She knew and they knew they just wanted to buy a home right now and they needed her help. Yes, of course buyers can go on the Internet now and do their own shopping, but they still need a good, reputable agent to help them with all the legal ramifications and represent them in the process.

Now sometimes these people would make an offer contingent upon seeing the inside of the house. To do this, my wife would e-mail all the hot new listings and tell them which ones she thought were a great buy. So the buyers trusted her advice and would go off of that to make an offer.

What a time saver! So, if you really do like working with buyers, why not try it this way? All you have to do is keep up on all the new, daily listings in the area that your buyers want. They will respect you more and it puts you in control.

She hardly worked weekends, too, unless it was such a great buy that she knew the house would be sold by the following Monday.

So the last number to look at is total closed, which was 87 for the year. We did it in only 125 days. Not bad for a part-time agent, huh?

Could we have done 174 deals if we worked 250 days? Maybe. But let me tell you how much our lives improved because we did not work that many days.

- We went on more vacations.

- We attended our kids tae-kwon-do lessons and tournaments all the time.

- We volunteered at our kids' schools all the time.

The New Age Real Estate Agent

- We became community consultants for the high school kids (more volunteering).

- We donated money to more things that we believed in.

- I learned to play the piano after buying a nice, big grand piano – something I always wanted to do.

- I spent more time with my wife in the afternoons when nobody was at home!

- I competed in bicycle racing.

- I got my pilot's license back and flew again.

- I spent more time with my kids.

- I learned how to draw and oil paint (decorating our home with huge, 4' by 6' canvasses that I actually painted).

And the list goes on…

The point is, I had way more time to do the things I really wanted to do in life and live the life of my dreams.

So decide on the following to begin your dream life:

1. How many days a week do you want to work and actually be there committed 100% to make a difference?

2. How much money do you want to make?

3. How much time do you want to spend with your family? If you are single, how much time do you want to be single?

4. Do you want to work part-time and focus the other time on another business? (highly recommended)

5. What do you want your life to look like in three to five years? In 20 years?

6.   What do you want your health to be like in three to five years? In 20 years?

7.   How much money or time do you want to give to charity or another useful cause?

8.   How much of yourself do you want to give to helping others have a great life?

The New Age Real Estate Agent

Chapter 9

Handling Fear

"We are all the same; we are either running away from pain or moving toward pleasure at any given point. That's what gives us the balance in life. Ask yourself, are you running toward your dreams daily?"

Tom Hale

Fear is one of the most, if not **_the_** most, goal stopping, life stopping, backwards thing that can hold you back in all areas of your life. Fear itself is the opposite of love. If you go through life being fearful, then that's what you will attract. If you go through life full of love, compassion and understanding, then that's what you will attract.

Let me give you an example here. Let's say you are on the phone cold calling around, looking for listings. The person answers the phone and you say, "Hello! My name is _____ and I am with _____ company. Would you like to sell your

The New Age Real Estate Agent

home?"

Then the person screams, "No, jerk! Don't ever call me again!"

Why did that happen? Well there are a number of reasons.

1. You came from a point of taking.
2. Why would they want to tell you that they were selling, even if they really did?
3. There was fear in your voice and they could sense it.

Here is a better scenario. Let's say you target market an area. You are well known in that community for giving to the local schools, donating your time and energy to good causes there. You go into the local grocery store and people recognize you and automatically trust you. They come up to you and ask you about real estate and what the market is doing. You are happy that people know you (recognition to feed your ego) and that you can truly help them with questions. Your name is spoken and everyone gets quite and listens.

A person that you met two months ago comes up to you at the grocery store and asks you some questions about real estate and then tells you that they want to purchase a home in that area and they are serious about making a move as soon as you can find them something. Then you go to the phone or to the doors and ask around and truly help them out.

Here is how I do it now when door knocking: "Good morning! My name is _____ with _____ and I have a buyer that wants to purchase a home in this area. Have you given much thought to moving lately?"

Then they answer, "Well, actually we have been thinking of it," Then they tell you more about things as they open up to you. So why did it happen this way versus the first way?

The New Age Real Estate Agent

1. You came from a point of giving versus taking as in the first case.
2. The universe and God rewarded you for being honest because you truly did have someone.
3. You said it with a smile on your face and energy exuding from you.

So, in short, you build it and they will come. That is, of course, you build your business on the principals of love, giving, honesty and integrity.

Fear itself is defined in the dictionary as frightened, to feel fear in oneself, to be afraid of, expect with alarm intransitive senses; to be afraid or apprehensive. All of these words make me cringe!

Is this living life? Do you not feel best when you are going for it daily? Isn't it about the journey? Fear's job is to protect you from making bad decisions or to make good ones. So, in a sense, it really is great that we have this emotion called fear. Because without it, wouldn't we all just be these superstar people achieving everything daily? Probably, but where would the excitement be?

So since we know this, why not use it to our advantage? For your mindset, you could use it like this example:

I used to be very fearful of cold calling or door knocking for business. Once I understood that it was not just me that was fearful and I knew other real estate agents out there felt the same as me, then things felt better. I also knew that I and other agents had to be aware of this and to use it to my advantage. I use to pull up in my car to the neighborhood that I was going to door knock and just sit there for a bit and if a drop of rain touched my windshield, I would have the excuse not to go out. That was kind of hard because everyday was like that where I lived. So I would make myself go based upon my integrity that I had with myself. I made a promise that I was going to visit so many houses that day and week. Then I thought of all the other agents that would not even have made a commitment like that, let alone do it and a smile would come to my face as I walked up to the first door and rang the bell.

Then I had to get over the fear of what was on the other side of the door 150 times a day. Sometimes, it was not pleasant. But the way I presented myself really deflated people's emotions. I dressed nice and casual and very clean cut. I always thought about the people who in the past knocked on my doors growing up. Most of these people were dressed in shabby clothes and missing some teeth. Most of them (or all of them) wanted something from me. So they came from a point of taking, **not giving**.

When I door knock for real estate, I come from a point of giving because I give them some useful information about the market and let them know if they ever need my help, to just call. Think of all the people who have knocked on your door in the past – they all wanted something from you, right?

- Politicians for your vote - now
- Landscapers to cut your lawn – now
- Book clubs that want money – now
- People from the poor side of town that turned their life around and need your money – now
- All the rest

So this itself is a big fear that developed in my mind. The fear of what people thought of me as I rang their doorbell.

When learning to fly airplanes at the age of 16, of course I was afraid. But my goal then was to first learn how to solo on my own. On my 10th time out with my instructor after we made a safe landing and sat there on the runway with the engine running, she surprised me by opening the door of the plane and quickly stepping out. The engine was still loudly running with the propeller turning and slicing the air. It was so loud, she yelled to me, "I want you to do three touch and goes on your own," as she shut the door to the plane and ran off leaving me so alone. She did look back at me and gave me an assuring wink with a head nod as she raised her eyebrows.

I thought to myself, "What the &*%&*"! I have never done this before. Is she crazy?" My heart beat a million miles per hour as I sat in that plane and looked out to the lonely runway and all could hear was the loud and scary propeller. I had two options; I could shut the engine off and do it some other time, or I could trust my instructor that she had confidence in me to do this in the first place. Wasn't she the professional here?

I decided to go for it and believe me it wasn't a Yeehaw kind of go for it. It was more like a, "Oh, ^%$&*! I hope I live!"

My hand was shaking so hard I could barely hold onto the yoke. I took off pretty fast because her weight was not there (she was skinny, too). Then I remember her on the radio talking to me as she was preoccupied eating something. She mumbled with a mouthful, "I can see you….. you're doing great. Now don't forget to pull the carburetor heat when you make the final turn." I answered back in a voice that only came from my mouth because the rest of my body was stiff as a board, "Six niner mike, roger."

Then came the runway in sight as I made my first final turn. It was all clear with no other planes on it. I was coming in too high and the muffled instructors voice came on, "You're too high!"

"Yeah, no %&it, Sherlock," I thought to myself. So I put

the nose down to compensate, but that just made the plane come in faster! I did not care as long as I came onto the runway. So the next thing was me hitting the concrete pavement so hard that the plane bounced up and never went back down, so I decided to make it look as if I planned it that way....yeah, I planned it that way because it was a touch and go that I was supposed to do! I can only think of situations like this where you are all alone and you are praying that you will live. It's just your God and you.

Anyway, the next two landings came in perfect and I remember pulling the plane in off the runway after I made my final landing and she was still inside the flight office eating and reading something. I shut the engine off and got out as my legs were pure rubber. Where was she? Wasn't she going to come running out screaming, "You stud! You made it!"

No, she just acted like it was just another day in the life of a flight instructor where they think they are God. Maybe it was good that she did not come running out, because my confidence level actually increased because I felt she believed in me so much. Maybe she planned to act that way so as not to blow any confidence I had in myself – who knows?

What was great was that I didn't think about it too much (I wasn't in that position), so I just went for it when she left the plane. After that, I was hooked to come back for more lessons.

So, this is where my part of my confidence came from. It wasn't and hasn't been that I am just that type of person that has no fear. I have just as much as anyone else, it's just how I choose to deal with it.

As Mel Gibson in the movie "Braveheart" said in his speech to all the clan before the battle at Sterling, "Would you be willing to trade all the days that followed from here forth, while you are lying comfortably in your warm beds and knowing that you could have had your freedom for **this one day?**" He said this as they wanted to go home and just settle for a life that was given to them by a king and not what they truly wanted.

I ask you, likewise, do you really want to make a difference in your life? Who knows what's at the end. But wouldn't you rather try your hardest and feel good about living life to the fullest instead of settling for mediocrity? Quit playing small; everyone around you is doing that. If you won't, then move over and get out of the way for the people like me that want to make a difference while we are alive on this planet.

So remember, fear is just an emotion to be controlled. So by coming up with a plan of how you want your life to be and having the integrity everyday to do what you say you will do, no matter what your dreams will come true with a little less fear every day.

The New Age Real Estate Agent

Chapter 10

Making All Presentations in The Office

"To believe in oneself is easy; to make the first step is hard."

Unknown

What would you think of if I told you that I did all my presentations in the office – all the listing and buyer presentations? Would you say, "There is no way!" Would you think it was possible to list a home without ever seeing it?

This is what I do now and let me tell you about it and how exciting it is!

What a time saver for both you and the client!

First of all, let me list all the advantages. Doing this:

1. Saves time and energy for both you and the client
2. Saves you gas

The New Age Real Estate Agent

3. Allows you to price a property more realistically
4. Allows you to be in control and not them (key issue)
5. Allows them to see your office and how professional you and your staff are
6. Allows them, when they come into your office, to go online with you and even tell you which properties they want to look at (giving them a sense of control)
7. Lets them not lose total control of the situation and be able to make a sound, educated decision

I always ask other agents why they need to go to the client's house to take the listing. It is always the same response. They look at me while they look around, searching for an answer. I think this process is so far out there that nobody has thought about it. "Why do you really need to go over there to their house?" I ask them. Then the agent's response is, "Well, you have to see the house, don't you?" My response then is to say, "You personally can if you want, but why not send someone else like a home stager over?"

Is it because tradition has always said that's the way it should be? Is it because the client wants it this way? Is it because you have to see what you are selling? Is it because you want to build rapport with them? What is it!?

Here is how I do it and I hope to answer all those questions and any you might have in your mind right now. When I get a call from a potential client that wants to list their home, the conversation will go like this.

The New Age Real Estate Agent

Potential New Listing Script

Agent: Hello, this is _____ with _____. How can I help you?

Seller: I was interested in a market analysis on my home.

Agent: Great! Whom am I speaking with?

Seller: My name is Lisa.

Agent: Well Lisa, thank you for calling. Are you going to be moving soon? And if so, where to?

Seller: Well, we are getting a job transfer to Texas and will be moving in the next two months. Can you come over and tell us what our house is worth?

Agent: Great Lisa! Can I share with you how I work?

Seller: Yes, go ahead.

Agent: Well Lisa, instead of me coming over to your house with just one or two little pieces of paper to show you what your home is worth, I invite you and all the decision makers to come into my office. I have a big, flat-screen video monitor that is hooked up to the computer so we can both go online and see exactly what is happening in the market at that point in time. We will be able to see a number of photos of each comparable property to yours. This way we will be able to both objectively agree on a price that will cause your home to sell. Make sense?

Seller: Well…yes…that sounds good. How long does it take?

Agent: It will only take about 20 minutes, depending on how many questions you have. I do all my seller appointments between 3 p.m. to 5 p.m. Which do you prefer?

Seller: How about 5 p.m.?

Agent: Great! Now, before you go, can I ask a few questions about your property so I can be better prepared for you?

Seller: Yes.

The New Age Real Estate Agent

Then I would ask more questions like:
- How much she owes
- How big the house
- Does she need a new loan
- How much she thinks it's worth
- And so on

If it sounds like the seller wants to be in control and asks extra questions, then use the rest of this script....

Seller: This all sounds great, but when are you coming out to see my home?

Agent: Great question, Lisa! Here is how we do it. After you come in and we agree on paper about the price and terms of the listing, I will send out my professional home stager at no extra cost to get your home ready to sell! She is licensed to do this and she will be going through your home room by room and will come up with a final checklist of what you need to do get top dollar for your home. You can use what you want and throw away the rest. But I suggest you take her full advice and do it all.

Seller: That sounds great! Can she come over before our meeting?

Agent: No, I am sorry, she will come out once we all agree that you will have your home on the market with us and let us sell it for you.

Seller: Is there an extra charge for that?

Agent: No, like I said, it is part of our great service that we offer to you at no extra charge. I have found that my properties sell a lot faster when I started doing this because my job is to sell your home, negotiate the offers, and keep the deal together...not home stage it and get it ready. That's my home stager's professional job.

Seller: Wow, sounds good!

The New Age Real Estate Agent

Agent: Great! Then I will have my assistant bring over some information that explains in detail how we sell homes in the area here. (Find out where the client is – home or office). Please take a few minutes to go over it, because it will save us a lot of time when you come over at 5 p.m. OK?

Seller: Sounds great!

Agent: Then I look forward to seeing you tonight at 5 p.m. Oh, by the way! Can you bring an extra key to your home when you come over please? Great! See you then!

This script works great and let me tell you why.

- It covers everything, including pricing the home correctly which the key issue you want to take care of.
- It is honest and not misleading.
- It puts you in control of the situation.
- The client automatically respects you and your professionalism.
- It gives you confidence and self-esteem the more you use it!
- It assumes the sale and the **close is natural** – no hard closes or trying to convince people about anything except how you do business.

I've had a few people that simply will not come to my office. They wanted me to see their house first.

I do not do this anymore and I will tell you why.

- I've made a *commitment* of how I run my business and now it is a habit.
- The people that wanted me to go to their home first have always been the ones that want to be in control. In the

end, I was more mad at myself for giving in to them and not staying in control (which is where you need to be, as any successful agent will tell you).

- They want to price it at their price and want to be in total control because they do not respect agents.
- It is a big red flag that pops into my mind when the seller insists that I go over first. They usually want to sell me on their price.
- They want to show me about the $75,000 they just spent on their new, fancy drapes for one window (don't laugh, it happened!) or whatever reason.

The Next Step: The Meeting

Since Lisa is planning to come into my office at 5 p.m. and it is now 9 a.m., the first thing I will do is to send my information of all the homes that I have recently sold in the area and other information about my business to her as promised. Then I ask my assistant to pull up all information on her home – past listings, tax role, property search through title company to see who is on title. After that, my assistant will type a listing contract and get all the paper work ready to have them sign when they come in. Everything is highlighted in yellow, so all I have to do is put it in front of them so they can go through and sign it.

At 4:45 p.m., I do some homework on their property for them before they come in. I have a big, flat-screen TV monitor in my conference room that is hooked up to the Internet. I go through and just familiarize myself with her street and neighborhood (I usually know because I am the area expert anyway). I do this so there are no surprises when she comes in.

At 5 p.m., she comes into the front door of the office

The New Age Real Estate Agent

where she is professionally greeted by my assistant who hands her a clipboard (questionnaire) and a bottled water. My assistant energetically says, "Hello! Tom is expecting you. Can you please have a seat and fill this out? I will let Tom know you are here."

At 5:05 p.m., the seller completes the questionnaire and my assistant gives it to me in my back office while she stays up front – just like a doctor's office. I read the questionnaire and look at her responses to the questions. Then I go out and greet her, then bring her back to the conference room where I offer her more water or coffee. If she has kids, there is a small TV for watching kids' videos and crayons with paper to keep them occupied.

I then get right into showing her comparable homes on the Internet and tell her that I was just doing my homework for her on her property right before she came.

Around 5:20 to 5:30 p.m., we both then agree on a realistic price that will cause the home to sell and then she signs the papers! She also has brought the key to her house and gives it to me. Of course, if she has any questions, I will answer all of them to the best of my knowledge. I then shake her hand and walk her out.

After that, I give the key and the signed papers to my assistant and have her go through the "New Listing Checklist." I also give all the information to my home stager and have her call the seller to set up a meeting ASAP. Done!

If you look at it as total time spent on that one listing, it comes to less than one hour of my time to take this listing! That's:

- 10 minutes for the first phone call when she called in
- 15 minutes for me to prepare for her before she came in
- 30 minutes to present and sign listing

The New Age Real Estate Agent

Total: 55 minutes!

So ask yourself, how much total time and money are you spending to take one listing? Even if you have an assistant do most of the work, this is what you are likely doing:

- ❖ You have to drive to the listing appointment, with gas and the stress of driving to deal with.
- ❖ Maybe not taking the correct information over to the potential client (don't laugh, it happened to me).
- ❖ You spend energy on trying to say the right thing to impress them and have them like and trust you – in other words, building rapport.
- ❖ If you set the appointment at 5 p.m. and it takes 30 minutes to get there and another hour at their house to a signed listing (because they have to show you every nook and cranny) and 30 minutes to get back, if you are lucky you get to walk into your home and have your wife greet you with a frown at about 7 p.m. saying, "You missed dinner again. The kids ate your big piece of chicken. When are you going to get control of your life and have a normal job?"
- ❖ You spend more time and energy, which equals money and time, that you could spend with your family, learning a new hobby, going out on your yacht or taking more listings – you choose!

It is all mindset and how you want it to be, by visualizing it first with my help. If your goals and dreams are that powerful, then they will help pull you to them.

Chapter 11

It's In Your Schedule or It Doesn't Get Done

"I'd rather see a sermon than hear one any day; I'd rather have one walk beside me than merely point the way."

David O. McKay

I could just let the title of this chapter be all there is and write no more pages! It's true, if it's not in your schedule, then it will not get done unless you are lucky.

Do you want to run a business on happenstance? Do you want to run it on the way you *feel about things?* Do you want to be ordinary and in rapport with everyone else that makes excuses daily as to why they did not have enough time to exercise, to play with their kids, to love their spouse, to look for business, etc…(Yes, I did say "Love your spouse!")

The New Age Real Estate Agent

Some people ask me how you schedule spontaneity. Well, you just do and it's a lot better than not putting it in your schedule. Here are a few examples: my wife and I schedule date nights. We also schedule time to be alone where nobody can see us. We also schedule family time with kids and vacations, of course. I would rather have it in my schedule that my wife and I are going to be with each other on a certain day than not, because it keeps the momentum going of knowing that we will actually get this time together. This definitely makes our marriage better, too. If I don't have even the fun, spontaneous things in my schedule, then how can I ever touch on those things?

The other side to that is not putting them in your schedule and hoping that you will someday, somehow, when you feel like it, learn to play the piano or some other thing you have always wanted to do. I have it in my schedule everyday to play the piano from 1:30 p.m. to 2:30 p.m. and work on what my teacher taught me on our last session together. This is the perfect time, because nobody is home with no distractions.

Now to go a little deeper and schedule creativity is even harder, because creativity is something that usually hits you when you are hearing a song or looking at a beautiful sunset or whatever. So I put it in my schedule to oil paint on Saturday mornings when everyone is asleep and I can go into my studio with nobody around and start painting. How do I schedule creativity for that?

I know and tell myself all week long that I am a great painter and I read inspiring books on Van Gogh and Da Vinci. I get pumped up all week long and visualize myself painting a masterpiece and people offering me $50 million per painting! So when the time comes (not 100% of the time, mind you), I pick up the brush and am excited to express myself because I have an end dream. Sure, sometimes I have to drag myself in there to the studio, but that feeling always goes away after about two minutes and I remember my dream and the reason why I am doing it. The next time when I feel like that, I just remind myself.

I also have a great support system behind me and that's my wife that bugs me all the time as to when I am going to finish some certain project. OK, now I can hear a lot of you saying things like, "I don't have an art studio," "I don't have a spouse that supports me," "I don't have this or that." Well, I did not have any of these things before either and we all have to start somewhere, don't we? You only live once, as you know.

I think for my wife and I and the close friends that we have, we grow together. We have the same interests in life, well, not exactly – she doesn't paint or play piano or bike race or fly. But we do ballroom dance together and compete against other couples. We have a great time doing this together and learn a lot from each other. We set goals to be in certain dance competitions and that's what drives us to show up for our lessons. So when it comes time to show up for our lessons, it's easy because we talk about our goals. Or if one does not feel much energy in it at lesson time, then the other picks them up and says, "Look, we came here. Let's get it done!" So we feed off each other's energy and it always seems to work out as long as we keep setting goals and looking at them. Also, it's quite easy to look at our dancing goals now because there are so many TV shows on the subject to watch. We actually started ballroom dancing in 2000.

We also have the same family goals, the same goals to be in shape, the same goals to give to the community, the same investment goals and so on. We go to seminars together and have always learned at the same pace in life. This is called a life partner, wouldn't you say?

The New Age Real Estate Agent

I hear it all the time about a spouse that, "Just does not understand me." My reaction to that is try understanding them first. Get in their world, become involved with what they do, and walk in their shoes for a bit. They will definitely respect you more for it and then it will come back to you ten-fold.

Just like when you first met, you were very involved with each other and curious, right? Did you not tell each other vows at the marriage? Keep it going then and prove to the other that you are still that person! You have a job to do and that is always being the person that your spouse and kids believe you to be, so get over it and do it daily.

If you want it that bad – whatever it is – take control, take responsibility, and do it now! For gosh sakes, you're not getting any younger. Be thankful to your higher power for the tools you have to work with now, which include your hands, feet, ears, eyes and **passion** to live. A lot of people do not have some or all of these things and wish they did. Look at Christopher Reeves and how passionate he was before he passed away. He was on a mission to help other people and he did. I truly applaud him for that. I truly applaud his wife for all that she accomplished and the lives she touched also.

So by putting things in your schedule whether they are business, family, spiritual or hobbies, you need to have a dream for each one of those things, an end result that will pull you toward them. Remember what I keep saying, "If you don't have a dream, then your life will be about your problems." Make those problems simply tasks that you must get through in order to do what you need to do.

Make a schedule and stick to it daily – except have one day a week that you do not have one. It really is nice to be able to wake up whenever on that day and just lay in bed guilt-free if you

The New Age Real Estate Agent

want to. Me, I am always pumped with energy to do something! But at least have one day to reward yourself and your life will be great!

Start by putting it down in on a yellow pad, like so:

-5:30 a.m. rise and give thanks to be alive
-6 a.m. exercise
-7 a.m. get ready for day
-8 a.m. arrive at office and check in with assistant
-8:15 a.m. Role play with another powerful person and write affirmations.
-9 a.m. Look for new business and take a five-minute break every hour
-12 p.m. Lunch
-1 p.m. Return calls and do paperwork
-2 p.m. Appointments or look for more business
-4 p.m. Negotiate your offers and lead follow up
-5 p.m. Go home!

See how easy that is? I give you permission to run your business this way! Just stick to it, though. When you have things like someone wants to list their home and it's 10 a.m., what do you do? You tell them or have your assistant tell them that the only time available is between 2 p.m. to 4 p.m. When you are on the phone negotiating an offer and you know it's running past 5 p.m., then you better hurry and stick to your schedule. By the way, present all offers either over the phone or have the clients come into your office. Always tell them the truth about you having so much time to spend with them. This will keep them on track, too, and they will respect that you are a professional that has a schedule.

The New Age Real Estate Agent

Chapter 12

Taking Care of Your Customers by Knowing Them

"To know who you are, is to know others first."
Unknown

There are so many great books and written reports out there on how to give great customer service. It is up to you and what type of person you are or are becoming that will determine how your business will run.

My wife and I have dealt with a lot of bad agents that have made wrong choices and left us with holding the deals together ourselves. If this has not happened to you, then you better not put the blinders on because sooner or later it will.

The mindset we have now on this is to smile and know most people truly want to do good in life, but there are the ones that are jealous because they see you having it all. They will not admit they are jealous, of course, but will make up some excuse as to why a particular situation is the way it is. You know those people, right? It is those that do not take responsibility for their own actions and expect others to help them all the time; they like playing the victims.

Unfortunately <u>and</u> fortunately, we have them in our lives! What would life be without them? How could we learn and grow as people without them? Learning from these people is the best mindset to have. If and when something goes wrong in your business, you need to take full responsibility. Chances are that it was your fault in the first place. Admit it, say you are sorry, and move on. You might let your ego get in the way on that one and think that you will not let others take advantage of you. You are wrong; people take advantage of the weak in life, not the strong that are willing to admit their mistakes.

Basically, my wife and our team know that there are four basic personality types out there and by understanding these types we can better serve them on a more personal basis with great customer service.

The Analytical

These people are known for being organized, systematic and logical. They appreciate facts presented to them in a well thought-out, logical manner. They enjoy completion of detailed tasks and enjoy organization. They are sometimes viewed as too cautious and doing things too much by the book.   Weaknesses of the analytical involve being withdrawn, boring, quiet, reclusive and even sullen at times. If he or she seems indecisive, it's because of a need to assess all the data. Perfectionism can be a fault if the analytical pushes it too far. This person is definitely not a risk-taker.

The Amiable

These people are loyal, dependable and easy going. They are sensitive to the needs of others. They are sympathetic and empathetic and will offer their support to others without thinking too much about it. They "feel" a lot about things. Weaknesses include indecision and an inability to take risks. The amiable person is often too focused on others, conforming, quiet and passive. They often won't speak up for themselves, are too compliant and nice.

The Driver

These people are very competitive, demanding and assertive. They love the thrill of being in the action. They can do a lot in a very short time period and are often demanding. They focus on getting results. The driver is a high achiever – a mover and shaker who is definitely not adverse to risk. The individual is usually extroverted, strong-willed, direct, organized, forceful and decisive. Look for someone who tells it the way it is.

Watch out or you'll be worn down and bowled over by the driver, however. A driver is task-, rather than relationship-oriented person and wants immediate results. They can sometimes be over demanding, too, and unintentionally hurt others this way.

The Expressive

These people are very outgoing and enthusiastic with a high energy level. They are very social, charming and influential people. Sometimes slow to reach a decision, they are often thought of as impulsive, talkers and dramatic people.

Their weaknesses include impatience, a tendency to generalize, verbal assaults and sometimes irrational behavior.

Don't worry if you feel that you do not belong to any **one** particular group; I feel the same way. But there are studies that show we are usually one dominant type and when our back is against the wall under pressure, we convert to another type.

I am a driver. But when Lizbeth and I disagree and have words, then I usually shift to the analytical who tries to reason things out – which only drives her more crazy.

Now Lizbeth, on the other hand, is an amiable true to the heart. She is very soft spoken and "feels good about things." She is very sympathetic and she supports any and everyone. But when we fight, she gets to be the total expressive with the name calling and screaming included – not to mention things becoming airborne!

So just understanding this little bit between her and I sure has saved our marriage more than once. We often talk between us about what if we were both drivers or both amiable. We always come up with the same conclusion and that is it simply would not work out. I like being in control and sometimes (Lizbeth says all the time) demanding. There is no way I could be around anyone in a relationship that is that type for a long period of time.

Now, when it comes to my business or just people on a daily basis, it is a different story and I put my feelings aside. Most of us do this. At that time, I know that I need to be flexible and get along with them. (My mom did teach me some things, after all.)

Think about the people in your life right now that are very stubborn and they don't get along with too many people. These people really could get along with others if they were just more flexible. But to know more flexibility requires the learning of how others are and why they are that way.

Study these four different types and you can go a long way with your customers. Go through everyone right now that you know and write down on paper what type they are and why you think they are that type.

A perfect example of a customer that I used to lose the listing on sometimes was the analytical type. The person (usually the engineer, the math teacher or someone in a facts field) would meet with me and have to have all the facts and I mean _all_ the facts presented to them as to why I came up with a particular price to list their home on. Sometimes, I just wanted to beat my head against the wall and scream at them, "You're thinking about it too much! Just sign the contract!" I would get upset sometimes and think that I was not closing the right way or they just did not like my presentation or whatever. That is, until I started reading people better and studied these types. Only then did I realize it was just all my fault for not letting that person be who they really were.

The analytical wants facts and figures; they are usually emotionless and sometimes treat you like you are beneath them for not being as smart as them. So now that I know this, I try to see what type of personality they are before we meet at my office. I ask questions like:

"Before you come into the office for our appointment, I would like to be best prepared for you so…"
- ➤ What type of work do you do? (This is usually the best and will tell you what type of person they are – like an engineer usually is an analytical)
- ➤ Do you like to see a lot of facts and graphs?
- ➤ How do you make your decisions? Do you bounce things off others first? Do you have to feel a certain way before making a decision?
- ➤ Describe a business situation you were in that you did not like and why.

Most people love to talk about themselves and want to tell you these things. It's a win-win situation because you are really listening to them as to who they are and they like that. So don't think of it negatively like you are manipulating them. Do you manipulate your partner? Your mom? Or anyone else in your life? Or do you communicate the best way you can with them for a positive outcome.

I customized my questions to fit me because the quiet analytical is the worst one for me to deal with (or should I say to be flexible with). So now with the analytical type, I know that they want facts and figures and need time to make a decision. Sometimes it's not for days. But I keep following up until I get the listing.

Lizbeth and the rest of our team is always using this process now. Our assistants use it when they have to talk to our clients. We even put a note in their file as to what personality type they are and it really helps!

The New Age Real Estate Agent

Sometimes when we can't figure out what type they are, then we might have a meeting and everyone gives their input as to why they think they are that way.

This provides great customer service to your clients and they love it that you care enough to get to know them more on a personal basis.

So my final advice on great customer service is give more than you take, under-promise and over-deliver!

The New Age Real Estate Agent

Chapter 13

You Get What You Attract

"Wherever you go, go with all your heart."
Confucius

I'm so excited to come to this chapter because it may be the most important one. We are all humans and we have what we have to work with. Why is it that some of us achieve great things in life, while others simply struggle? We all are human with mostly the same tools at our hands to work with, the same number of hours in a day. We are just on different levels.

For example, the rocket scientist at NASA has a few more tools than the teenager with her chemistry set in her garage. It's, of course, different levels.

Energy and Attraction

It has been proven that the universe is not only expanding, but as it expands it is also accelerating at the same time! The Hubble Space Telescope in its numbered days was pointed to a deep part of space. It was pointed to an area about the size of a dime at a distance of 75 feet away. They stared at the same spot in the sky for 10 days, taking photo after photo. The exposure time typically was 15 to 40 minutes per photo. What they saw amazed the seasoned veterans. They found at least 1,500 galaxies that were approximately 10 billion years old in just that one tiny, tiny area. So in reality, they were looking back in time 10 billion years and seeing the formation of galaxies.

If you look at the universe in its whole, then take it down to our galaxy, then take it down to our solar system, then to earth, then to you, then to your cells, your molecules, your atoms, then to pure energy, it's pretty amazing. If you look at your arm, you might say there is skin and under the skin there are tendons and bone and then atoms. But what are atoms made of? What is the chair you are sitting on made of? What is the paper of this book and the ink made of? Energy! That's it! It is pure, simple energy.

You have enough energy in you to light up a whole city for a week. Energy is moving into form and out of form at all times, whether you accept it or not.
We are all connected with each other. It's just one huge energy field.

When someone dies, where does the energy of that person go to? Does it just die with the person? Are the person's thoughts still alive and flowing through time and space? Is that person's energy still going strong, even if they are not?

I don't know all the answers, but my point is that we are all working with one infinite power of energy. And you become what you think about most. If you want to be a great, top-producing real estate broker, then that's what you will be. If you think about struggling as a real estate broker that just gets by, then that's what you will be. Your thoughts become reality.

Scientists have found that thoughts have different frequencies. A negative thought is on a different frequency then a positive, empowering thought. So whatever thoughts you keep thinking about, whether good or bad on a consistent basis, you will attract. Just like if you have low self-esteem and a lot of negative thoughts, you will attract bad things and bad people around you because they are on the same frequency or wave length. If you want a new car, to find your soul mate, or to achieve great health, all you have to do is keep thinking about them. You are like a huge magnet.

Attraction itself has no boundaries and it will give you what you deserve whether you want it or not. It just responds to your thoughts, actions and wishes. When you get mad at a client because they did not list with you or even give you the time for an interview, it is your fault, not theirs. You attracted that to yourself because of your thoughts. And the madder you get, the more energy you put out there and then the more it comes back to you.

If you want to be a great real estate broker, great spouse, or great friend, you need to affirm it with a yes! Then you open the door to it coming back to you through attraction. When you say, "No!" about something – a stubborn teenager, a client that is very difficult and so on – you are not pushing it away from you, but only attracting more of the same in your life. So choose

The New Age Real Estate Agent

carefully what you want and be wise.

When I was in grade school, I used to have a lot of girls writing me notes and asking me to put a list in order of who I liked the most. I was a pretty popular kid that had high self-esteem because I believed it. People told me I was a good-looking, handsome young man and that I had a lot going for me. I did not doubt myself and had many friends.

Then came junior high and everything about how I viewed myself changed. Some people said I had a big nose; some people said I was stupid. I started believing these people and their view of me. My self-concept changed. Crazy! Then in the eighth grade, I needed the connection of people so I started hanging out with the wrong crowd. We were about 15 strong. My identity of myself changed all the time, depending how the crowd thought and acted. At that time, I did not believe I was this handsome young man that was going places, but rather a street fighter that was out to prove how tough he was. I became what I thought about most with all the negative frequencies around me. I got into fist fights with guys twice my size, just to prove how tough I was. In one of my first fights, the other guy broke my nose and I had to have it operated on to re-brake it back in shape!. My mom could not believe what happened and nursed me back to health. My friends in the gang nicknamed me "Psycho" because when I fought, I would do a Tasmanian devil on the guy and win no matter what his size was. I fought on average once every month and was pretty confident because that's what my identity was at the time. I only lost one fight (my last fight). This guy beat me from one side of the street to the next. He gave me two black eyes, broke two blood vessels in my eyes, gave me a broken nose again and smashed my head on the hood of my own car. Yes, I said the hood of my own car! Then he left me for dead in the parking lot with my girlfriend holding me and crying. **I deserved it and had it coming.**

I guess this energy was better than no energy at all, so that's why I stayed in the group – stupid me.

I remember making eye contact back then with my old grade school friends and I could just tell what they were thinking. There were no girlfriends like the ones I used to have, not even close. Of course, being in a group of about 15 guys and a few girls, their opinion was everything to me and so jealousy was a major factor. All in all, I got what I thought about, which were bad things and bad people.

I had to actually move out of town and start on my own to get out of it all. At that time, I had started to wonder about human behavior and was asking myself some real important questions like, "What makes some people successful and others not?" and "Who am I?" and "Why do people have different identities?" "Is it because of their role models?" I also asked myself probably the most important one of all, "Can I change my identity or am I born into what I am now?" After reading a lot of self-help books, my answer to that question was, yes, I can change my identity and so can you. We can do this through our beliefs.

So if I believe that I am a handsome young man that is going places in life, then that is my reality. If I believe that I can make a billion dollars a year and give most of it away, then that's my reality and identity, too.

You are a magnet and everything that is brought to you, you attracted. Stop focusing on what you do not want in your life and start focusing on what you **want**. You see the people that complain about their health all the time, they attract that because they focus on how bad it is. Then you see the people that talk about eating good food, exercising and living a healthy life – they have that, too. The couple that talks about a great marriage and finding their soul mate has them. On the contrary, the person that talks about no love life and always attracting the wrong person has that, too. We all attract everything to us like huge magnets.

I remember the first time I understood this, I was afraid of my own negative thoughts. Know that a good thought or a affirmative thought is 1,000 times more powerful then a negative thought, so this will help cut down a little of the worry on your part. In reality, the thoughts we think of take a little time to manifest, which is a good thing. Remember those bad thoughts you thought about yesterday? Aren't you glad they did not come true?

I oil paint and I love it. The paint takes weeks to dry and I can actually go back the next day and work on something I don't like with just a few brush strokes. I believe the same is true for our thoughts; they are like the oil I use to paint with. There is no way to monitor your thoughts every second and you will go mad trying to do that. But there are ways that will help you be in the position to having more good thoughts – like hanging out with the right peer group, getting a collage together of positive images, writing daily affirmations, reading good books, only watching informative television, playing a musical instrument and so on.

On the other hand, the opposite is true, too. Have you ever seen a gang member that oil paints, plays the piano, and smiles all the time? Neither have I! You can always tell where a person is headed by looking at the friends they surround themselves with.

You have heard it said before that you are the sum of everything you have done prior to this moment. But also realize that you are the reality of your own thoughts. Once you really get this, you can go around saying to yourself, "It's my fault, it's my

The New Age Real Estate Agent

fault. The reason my life is the way it is today is because it's my fault!"

Whether you have great friends, your teenager runs away, you live under a bridge or you live in a mansion, **it's your fault!** Once you get into the habit of realizing this on a daily basis, then your life will never be the same again. It does not matter who you are in this world, it is the same for everyone. Just keep realizing this and know it is the truth and accept it. Do you have to understand why something works before you use it? Or can you just trust this? You do not have to know how your heart actually works in order to be alive, do you? You just trust it because it always produces the same strong beat.

Most people are good at thinking about what they don't want, not what they want. The things they don't want keep showing up over and over again – no listings, no sales, mean people, etc...

Whatever you are focused on and committed to feeling good feelings about, you are attracting to yourself on a daily basis. It also has to make sense with who you are, what you want and what you are going for. It all has to line up with how you feel about it and how committed you are to it, too, then the results come even faster. But if you feel bad about the thing or things you want and are doing, then you are out of sync with it all and it may never come or it will just take a lot longer coming.

Take, for example, a rose bush that you are taking care of and wanting it to produce some beautiful roses. If you talk to it, water it, fertilize it, and take care of it daily, then you will produce some beautiful roses. But, on the other hand, if you talk negative to it, and never water it or fertilize it, then you are out of sync with it and it will not produce anything – and if it does, it will be ugly.

The New Age Real Estate Agent

Pick you careers and your hobbies with great care and a loving heart, because if you get into something and are out of sync with it, it will take way more time then you think. I will use real estate, for example. I got into it for all the wrong reasons. I just wanted to make a great living at selling something, so I chose a commodity like homes because everyone needs them and the commissions are a lot bigger then furniture or food. I was out of sync the first few years in selling homes because it really wasn't me to be a salesman – I guess I was too nice. But it wasn't until I started doorknocking on my segway and having all my appointments come into the office that I was totally in sync with everything and then the money finally flowed in. I was doing it my way and having fun!

It's funny how some of the other coaching companies want to take credit for my successes, but they do not realize this one important thing and that is, I did it without them. Of course, they were inspiring, but nobody and I mean *nobody* can ever look into your own heart!

So by eating right and living a healthy lifestyle you are going to be in more sink with what you want and what is attracted to you. You can't feel bad all the time and attract good things, it just does not happen like that.

If you feel good and have a big dream and affirm it daily, then you are in a better position to attract that dream to yourself. This also means taking care of yourself physically, mentally and spiritually to be the best you can be while attracting your dreams.

Your Body

What more can we say about your body with so many great books out there focusing on eating, exercising and living a healthy lifestyle. If you do not treat your body with the respect that it deserves, then it will retaliate.

Let's just go over the simple truths here and get back to the basics, with no magic answer. Since our bodies are made up of 70% water, wouldn't it make sense to eat a diet made up of 70% water-based food?

For instance, whatever you eat, make it a point to eat 70% of that meal in water-based foods, like fresh fruits and vegetables.

Think of what are water-based foods: carrots, celery, tomatoes, spinach, lettuce, broccoli, apples, grapes, watermelon, oranges, etc. Pretty simple, right?

People want to complicate this so much that they have to do food combining and calorie counting, this book's diet and that guru's magic answer, when the truth is so simple. Just eat healthy and in small portions.

If you have a big family like I do and sometimes you have to eat fast food, then there are plenty of fresh sandwich delis out there to choose from. The point is just get in a habit of eating healthy and in small portions, because that really is the magic answer to it all, nothing more.

Another no-brainer is to *exercise daily* or at least six days a week for at least an hour at high intensity! I know all the latest books and reports tell you to exercise 20 minutes a day at least three days a week. But seriously, how can you begin to even get break a sweat in 20 minutes? What a joke!

The New Age Real Estate Agent

I mix up my workouts all week long; one day I will swim laps, the next I will ride my bike outside, the next I will lift weights, the next will be running outside and so on. I sign up ahead of time for triathlons so I am forced to keep in shape. My ultimate goal is to do an Ironman Triathlon. I have always said, the only tattoo I would put on my body is of that and the year I did it in. Then after each successful year of doing it, there will be the year of completion added.

The Ironman world championship triathlon is a 2.4-mile swim, a 112-mile bike ride and a 26.2-mile marathon run. Yes all on the same day. There are about 21 of these events all over the world at different months of the year now. I do triathlons now and have signed up for the new 70.3 Ironman, which is half of the swim, bike and run. I have a dream and attainable goals to get there, so I can see the finish line already.

I train for at least one to two hours a day because I really feel the human body needs to be in good condition to perform well on a daily basis. Not only that, but it really humbles a person, too. Plus, you will get the really deep sleep you need!

Sleep is Good

Which brings me to my next point and that is sleep. Get plenty of it. Put it in your schedule to nap for a half hour in the afternoon. Find someplace in your home or a quiet part of the parking lot or wherever so you can just close your eyes and rest! Put it in your schedule. Some of us are so driven to get to our day and do our schedule that we do not sleep enough. Hey, life is too short to be going through the day cranky and grumpy from lack of sleep, even if you are a millionaire.

The New Age Real Estate Agent

Now, on the other hand, if you do not exercise and you are tired, it is probably because you drink too much caffeine, eat a lot of white sugar, eat junk food and don't have a 70% water-based diet in fruits and veggies.

Look, this is not rocket science and I realize that sometimes we just need someone's approval to do it correctly...well, there you go, you have someone's approval now! So treat your trillion-dollar body with the respect it deserves!

If you don't have a healthy body, then it is really hard to do anything I have talked about in this book, like having the confidence to take listings at your price while they are in your office for the interview, or like having the energy to doorknock 100 to 200 homes daily and keep a smile on your face.

Getting sick and being unhealthy is a result of what I just talked about and stress. If you put enough stress on anything, it will fail. Our bodies create stress to let us know that our wheel of power is imbalanced.

The immune system is made to heal itself. Our body is the product of our thoughts. The human mind is the biggest factor in healing. Sometimes, when I get sick with the flu, I try real hard to fight it with my mind and then my fever gets even worse. But when I just give into it, knowing and believing that I will get better and let it flow like a stream, then my fever breaks.

The universe is abundant with pure, free-flowing energy all around us. Happy thoughts lead to a happy, healthy lifestyle. Since man becomes what he thinks about most, why can't a person be the product of their own happy thoughts?

How much opposition are you up against on a daily basis? A little? A lot? How much can you handle? How much do you throw out to others? Do you ever think about it or do you naturally conform to the way things are, just because you were raised that way?

Let me give you an example. When we were building our latest 9,000-square-foot home on an acre, we had plenty of space on the sides of the house for landscaping and my wife and I love to sample different types of wine, especially big, bold reds. So I thought to myself that both sides of the house would be great for growing grapes. I went out and bought a couple of books on the subject and, believe it or not, I had the perfect scenario for a small vineyard. The land was a perfect slope for the grapes to grow because they do not like a lot of water. The slope was facing southeast for direct sunlight in the afternoon and would have shade later in the day. The land was great for growing Pinot Noir grapes (red wine).

I did a little more research and found that we could easily get about 400 grape plants, which meant about 1,500 bottles of wine per year! (don't worry, we don't consume that much!) We then started daydreaming of opening up our own small wine-tasting business in the area where people could go in, sit, relax and be served as many different types of wine they wanted to try. Of course, ours would be one of them! Then we could sell the bottles to local patrons.

We then thought of a name for our wine and could visually see that I could oil paint a picture of grapes, then have it copied and use it for the label.

I went on the Internet and registered the new domain name. We also bought a new black lab puppy and named him *Vino* (wine).

When building our massive home, there were two huge crawl spaces, about 800 square feet each with a ceiling height of about 11 feet. The builder said he was not going to do anything with them and that's when Lizbeth and I asked him to make them rooms with hardwood floors. He OK'd it and added the extra

The New Age Real Estate Agent

rooms for us that we made into a gym and a wine cellar.
The builder had already made a wine room for us in a different
part of the house, but we needed a place to make the wine, so we
put in this wine cellar.

The wine cellar would be used for the making and
fermenting of the wine. I could see the whole family crushing
grapes in a big barrel with our bare feet and then getting into
grape throwing fights.

I did more reading on the subject of owning my own
vineyard and making the wine and I got more and more excited
about it. I am a person who loves physical labor and could see me
planting the posts and then taking care of the rows between the
grapes. So I hired a "grape guy," as I called him, to come over
and give me an estimate on what it would take for him to prepare
my land for the grapes. It did not come to that much, but he then
told me that all the nurseries in the area just ran out of my
particular plant and that I would have to wait until next year!

So right now, I am just getting the soil ready, and the
posts dug and put in perfect order so that when people drive by,
they will be able to see perfect rows of grapes on my land. I am
also learning how to make wine on my own with starter kits and
going through a lot of trial and error. I would rather make my big
mistakes while I can right now, instead of when it really matters.
The rooms are getting ready with the temperature and humidity
controls, too. You see all of this is so exciting to me because I
can actually see the end result of what I first dreamed of.

What is funny is that when I would tell any of the builders
here at the house of my dream, they would look me up and down
and say in a skeptical voice, "Have you ever made wine before?"
or "Have you ever done that before?" I then answered back, "No,
but there is a first time for everything!" and then I'd ask, "Did

you ever drive a car before you drove a car?" I then walked away smiling.

The quote at the beginning of this chapter is, "Wherever you go, go with all your heart." Well, let me tell you, that is what I have been doing most of my life. People like those builders will try to hold you back, of course. But they will try less if they do not know you and can't talk to you.

Whoever you are friends with, you will try to stay in rapport with each other and simply do the things the other does, whether great things or stupid things. I have found that I am alone most of my life, because there are not many people out there that want to do great things. Or, to put it more simply, there are a lot of great people out there, but they get held back by the rest that want to keep them there. But, thank you God, for Lizbeth because she is always right behind me in all of my decisions! We have done a lot together and what's so cool is that we are both growing together. Fortunately, we are both in the same field and get to dream together on the business side of things.

So, to sum it up, ask what your heart is telling you when you have to make those big decisions. As far as the little decisions everyday, you need to be running on autopilot of integrity and what your mom taught you. While I sit here in my gorgeous new home at my desk writing this, I am incredibly excited about life and what I have made of it. Not to mention, there is a picture of my daughter on my desk and I am listening to a beautiful CD of piano music. The house is quiet for now. My daughter's photo stares at me and silently hints as though to say, "I believe in you dad, you are perfect in my eyes." I try to be that perfect role model for my kids- because, for now, who else will be?

The New Age Real Estate Agent

So have the courage to follow your heart everyday in everyway. This is what you were intended to do. Your life and others around you will be richer for it.

The New Age Real Estate Agent

Chapter 14

Own It!

"What you think, you create; what you feel, you attract; what you imagine, you become!"

Unknown

What gets me is some of these so-called leaders around us that have never climbed the mountain, but said they have. They are good at talking and holding some of their seminars, but if you ask them how long they were in their profession, they can't give you an honest answer.

A lot of these people that teach and lecture now were unsuccessful in their field, so the next thing to do is to go out and teach! How can you learn from someone like that? Aren't you only learning what they have learned from others over the years? Probably.

Wouldn't you like to have your teacher teach you from his or her heart and soul, just like drill sergeants do? Think about them for a bit. Didn't they have to go through all the pain and misery to get where they are, through the gut-wrenching yelling, grunting, running up hills, helping others out, push-ups till they puked and not to mention the mental part – to get to where they are? Haven't they lived that life and have the power of owning it? They still do now and pass it on to others! This is what experiencing, teaching, and owning it are all about.

When people climb Mt. Everest, they are helped by the Sherpas. The Sherpas are the experienced locals that help the climbers out. They do this all the time and help out by carrying heavy loads and guiding. Khumbu glacier is at an elevation of 17,400 feet, and this is only base camp! Then you have four more camps ahead of you until you reach the summit of Mt Everest at 29,028 feet!

Of course, you can learn from the people who only go to base camp. Then you can learn from the ones that just make it up to the next four camps, but never made it to the top. But what about learning from the person that makes it to the top. You will learn it probably wasn't their first time. They were the ones before that only made it to base camp and then eventually got better and better. Or, if they did make it to the top on the first try, it was either sheer luck (I doubt) or they had help from others that knew the way and had experience.

These people own every level they have achieved; they can teach people every level they have achieved. Can you imagine talking to the person that *owns* the feeling and experience of making it to the top of Everest on a regular basis? What do you think they look and act like?

I can visualize them now; they breathe with confidence, slow and deep. They hold their head high, not to look down on anyone but to know they have done their best and that's a feeling nobody can take from them because they own it!

The New Age Real Estate Agent

How many times have you heard the phrase, "If you want to climb the mountain, ask the man who climbs it everyday?" How inspiring is that?

Can you imagine going to the bottom of a super huge mountain and looking up to it as you raise your eyes first, then your head follows as your mouth drops open? There you are with your Starbucks in one hand, brand new hiking boots that you paid $250 hard-earned dollars for (and by God the salesman told you they were the best!) on your tender feet, perfectly ironed shorts that have no stains (yet!) and your shiny new Rolex watch that you just purchased for your frail wrist.

Talk about being at the bottom of the mountain! You don't even own it yet. You're like a kid that is the last one to be picked for a team on the playground at recess.

Then the feeling really hits you in the stomach – pow! As you see the strong, confident, sure-footed mountain climbers coming down and walking by you with their heads high and grinning ear to ear, you notice they have healed scars from all the previous times they went up before as you look down at their broken-in hiking boots. They also have brand-new, open, bleeding wounds that they are very proud to show off. Some of them are limping, some are skipping, but most are just coming down with an air about them that nobody can take away. Glowing. Single file. They truly own it.

I wish I could see the majority of real estate agents like this. I'm so tired of seeing the agents that have the biggest and best cars and the fancy clothes. But take a look at what area they live in, their homes, their friends and especially their health. They walk around with this big ego (yes it is nothing more than an ego at this point, because that's all they have to go on) bragging about their last trip to Cabo to you. They live in a different reality.

The New Age Real Estate Agent

I say this in humor, but also in seriousness. It's not just agents out there, it's everyone! It's everyone that has never tried their hardest in something, or they have but gave up too early. Then after the storm cleared (or should I say, the little dust devil), then they say they own it. But in their own heart, they know they do not.

When you need to learn about a subject or when starting a new career, you <u>first</u> commit yourself – ***then and only then*** – gather all your resources and head straight for the best of the best teacher – someone who owns it!

Can you still own it if you just got to first base? You can if you *only* want to teach people how to get to first base; otherwise, you better not tell them how to hit it out of the park!

Look at it like this:

-If you get a ***poor*** teacher, then you will get ***<u>less</u>*** than poor results. Why less than? How can you do better than them? Luck, faith?

-If you get a ***good*** teacher, then you will get ***<u>less</u>*** than good results. Why less? How can you do better than them? Luck, faith?

-If you get an ***excellent*** teacher, then you will get ***<u>less</u>*** than excellent results. How can I do better than them?

-Now if I get an ***outstanding*** teacher, someone that is superior over the best (yes, they are out there), then at least you will get excellent results. Right?

What makes the outstanding teacher better than the excellent teacher? A fraction! That's it! We're talking a tenth of a second when it comes to the gold medal between Gold and Silver. But what made that person try harder to get the gold? It's really easy...heart and some simple truths that you should know.

These truths involve the basic elements that we have in

our daily lives. Some people call it the law of attraction, some call it God and faith, some call it the universe, and some call it their own religion. I call it **HEART** and the courage of following it.

The New Age Real Estate Agent

Chapter 15

Doing It All with Passion and Focus

"To live passionately daily is to know you can't live forever - only your legacy will."

Tom Hale

Why are you doing all of this? Well, 99% of this game is mindset. It's not about just making a lot of money, but living the dream and accomplishing all your goals in life at the same time. If you don't have a real reason why you are doing this (an end result), then your dreams will only half-manifest themselves and you will just be another statistic and lose your license and fail at it.

So what are your beliefs? Do you believe that you are entitled to an awesome life with everything you ever wanted? If you do, then that's what you will get. Do you believe that you should only get so far because that's what your parents, friends and peers said you should have? Then you are right, too!

If you showed me who your peers are, then I could tell you what lifestyle you have. If your peers are people that live at the poor end of town, then you will, too. If your peers are people that travel around the world, are well-respected and give to others, then you will, too. If your peers are people that always think at the highest level and are always bettering themselves, then you will, too.

But let me say this. There are more people at the low end of the spectrum than the high. You can see it for yourself. How many people live in the medium income part of town? The majority, that's who!
How many people live in the richest, most expensive part of town? Is it 5%, 10%, 3%? Who knows, but it's not the majority.

It is like this with your peers, too. The higher you go on the ladder of life, the fewer friends you have to relate to. So if you want to stay with the majority of the people and have an average life, then keep hanging out with those peers that do that, too. If you truly want to have the best and be your best in life, then choose those peers that want that, too. Careful though, there aren't too many people that are willing to do what it takes to be their best and it's easy to get sucked back into the old ways because you miss the unity and variety of your life.

Why can't you be someone who is consciously aware of this on a daily basis, someone who knows how life works and uses it to their advantage? The answer is because it's too hard for the majority. "It's not what I was meant to be," they say to themselves.

How do you know this? How do you know what the meaning in life is? Or better yet, what your meaning in life is?

The New Age Real Estate Agent

Aren't you at your happiest when you are achieving and truly going for it, when you are giving to others and there is love and understanding in your life?

Fake It Until You Make It

Sometimes the people I am coaching ask this really important question: "You tell me how to keep the dream alive, but what about keeping the motivation up?"

I always tell them the same thing. The answer is inside you. Quit looking for the answer to your motivation outside yourself. Meditate on it and ask yourself that very question – "Why am I doing this and how do I keep doing this without quitting?" After you answer your own question, then you will be truly more motivated to carry out the task or the long-term goal, because it came from *your* heart, not someone else's.

For example, when I was driving to the office today, I was stopped by a construction crew working on the power lines overhead. One of the power lines dropped to the ground right in the middle of the intersection just as I arrived. The situation did not look good because there was major traffic waiting to go through. So one of the workers on the ground took the initiative and stopped all the traffic with his hands so he could get to the line and take care of the problem. It looked as though he was going at fast speed to me and his other co-workers were moving in slow motion trying to help him. I could tell he knew what he wanted to do and knew the outcome, too, which was getting the power line off the street and letting the traffic move without any mishaps. The co-workers knew what had to be done, but they were not the ones taking charge like the first guy did, so they did

The New Age Real Estate Agent

not own the situation, thus running in slow motion.

So motivation comes from you taking control of what you are doing and knowing your outcome. Just because I write this great book on selling real estate and you read it does not make you do any of it. What makes you do any of it comes from inside your own heart. Because in the end, it is your life, not mine.

The other thing I tell people that I am coaching is to keep the fire lit under themselves. For example, I was complacent with my car. The lease was up and I wanted something different, something exciting and fun to drive! So I went to a luxury car dealer and started looking around. At first, I knew what my budget was to spend and I test drove this and that, but what I really wanted was sitting on the showroom floor! It was beautiful and the most expensive car in the whole dealership. It never even occurred to me to see what it would take to buy it.

After looking at some of my debts, like one of the maids that we really do not care for and another frivolous expense, I could see that it was possible.
After figuring out that I could do it came the next dilemma, and that was Lizbeth's acceptance of the idea itself. She said, "Aren't we humble people?"

"What is humble?" I asked with my arms in the air. So, as it turns out, my immediate motivation was to make that car payment, but now guess who is driving that beautiful car now? I'm not complaining, though -- she said yes to the new Porsche!

This was a great fire to light underneath us. Of course, we will find a way. We always do, don't we? But sometimes you have to do these things on a continual basis to keep your motivation and passion for life alive.

I have heard phrases like, "Fake it until you make it," "Live it like you are," and others. What is the difference of putting a smile on your face and knowing that your body will soon follow? Isn't it the same philosophy?

Every piece of real estate Lizbeth and I have ever purchased was never planned out. Of course, in the big picture of things, they were planned out because we have known how many houses we want to own and the financial freedom we want, too. But life just does not work like that. Once you understand how life works and that it was meant to be played full out with passion and emotion, the better off you are.

How boring would life be to know that tomorrow you would get this and that? And isn't it fun to buy a $365-million lottery ticket and dream with your family on how you would spend it – going through how your life would be, the people you could help, the things you would be able to do and so on. It's fun!

The Time Is Now

So when is the time right for you to actually go for it in life? Is it when things are just perfect and you have all the money you need? Is it thinking that you will feel better doing it after something happens? It never will. Now is the time to live life – today, this moment! Believe me, you can't have it all and you cannot take it with you. But you can sure die trying!

Start by taking up a new sport and competing in it. A few years ago, when Lance Armstrong was beginning to be a household name, I got into bike racing. It all started when Lizbeth decided to surprise me with a new Trek bike for my birthday. It was just like the one Lance Armstrong used to win the Tour de France in 2002. I got on that bike and rode it

The New Age Real Estate Agent

everyday for three months straight, then joined a bike racing team. I was head over heels for this new sport and nothing was going to get in my way. I rode with the team (about 40 of us) every Saturday morning and we rode anywhere and everywhere from 35 to 75 miles and even some century rides (100 miles).

It was a great experience and I was one of the oldest on the team at 40. The average age was probably about 25 and still in college. There were older guys than me and they did pretty well, too, because they used their wisdom and skills compared to the raw power of the younger people. But each age group fed and learned from each other.

Bike racing is the biggest team sport I have ever been involved in. When I started going out with the team at first, I was lousy on the hills. The team would take turns pushing me up the hills by putting their hands on my lower back and taking turns pushing me. If you never experienced this, then let me tell you what you are missing. When you are going up a steep hill and there is not one more ounce of energy in your legs to go further, and it feels you are ready to meet your maker, then all of a sudden someone comes up behind you and starts pushing you, you think they are God.

"How does this person have the energy and power to not only help me, but at the same time use only one hand on their own bike and still ride up the steep hill carrying themselves?!" It really humbles a person and shows what some people are made of. It wasn't long until I had the honor of helping others like this, too.

It was a cool experience to have the unity and passion of a team treat everyone the same. When we were done after a long, grueling ride, they would say to me, "Just keep coming back, Tom, it gets better every time!" I did keep coming back and then

The New Age Real Estate Agent

when I found I was the one to beat the team to the top of a major hill, I would come back down to the lowest rider and start pushing them up; it was what was expected of you since you had the power to do it.

Wouldn't it be great if agents did that? You never know the feeling of riding in a straight line two by two going 35 miles per hour until you experience it. If one person falls two or three rows up from you, there is a great chance that you are going down, and hard. The lead two people are the ones pulling the pack. They do this for a period of time until they get tired and then peel off to the back of the group. Then it is the next two people in line to pull for the group. It is always kept at a steady pace by mass communication within the group by everyone yelling things like, "Pick up the pace up front!" or "Slow it down, relax a little up there!" You are looked down upon if you get right to the front and chicken out on pulling because everyone is supposed to do their fair share, and that is not team work. Nothing is really ever said, but then you can tell from the energy of the team. Everyone knows.

When someone has a flat, they yell out real loud, "Flat!" and the message is carried to the front so they can slow down and eventually make a big slow turn and come back for the person.

Bike racing is a little like selling real estate. It is not a one-man operation. No man is an island, right? And when you put together your team that works for you, you have to treat it like what I just described. When one person on your team gets a flat, the leader still does what they are supposed to do but they slow down a little bit, not only for respect but to come back and help out. When someone is a rookie on the hills and needs help until they can do it on their own, then you push them from the back. There is lots of communication in the group and everyone knows what is happening at all times.

In bike riding with the team, the lead people have to point with their fingers and arms where a pothole is or something that could be dangerous to the group. That way everyone can steer around it without slowing down. Same thing in real estate or any business – the lead person has to communicate what they see up front and warn the rest of the team of any dangerous situations coming up.

Now this is all great in the Saturday training rides, but where it really pays off and gets exciting is on the races. The races could be 40 miles long and filled with 20 different teams of people that you do not know. You might have only four people that showed up for that particular race that is on your team. Then you have to communicate before the race and have a game plan as to how your team will win it. The fastest person usually gets the shot at the glory to sprint across the finish line at the end. They got this position because they deserved it and there is no arguing about it. It is the job of the others to make sure that the sprinter is protected throughout the race and given a clean shot at the finish by a set up. Remember, it is a team sport and everyone one gets what is deserved to them.

Real estate is the same way with a team. Why would you send a rookie on your team to do all the listing appointments when they have not earned the right to be there? It is the job of everyone on the team to make sure all the marketing was done on time, the bills paid on time, the lead follow-up done, etc. To set up the lead person or persons to take the listings or to sell buyers a home, everyone has a specific job that they need to perfect and then they can move up to the next level if they so choose to do so. The team will run at full efficiency when this type of mindset is understood and communicated within the team.

The New Age Real Estate Agent

A year ago, I crashed in a race and it stopped everything cold for a while. I was racing category 3 (1 is pro and 5 is beginner) and there was about 40 of us going around the track at 35 miles per hour. It was at a car racetrack and there was a concrete wall on the inside. I was next to it and about a third from the front. In bike racing, when someone at the front slows down by one mile per hour without even putting on their brakes, then by the time it reaches the very back, it is a full-on use of the brakes. This is called the accordion effect.

Likewise, if someone on the far left of the pack leans into the group, by the time it gets to the other side, it will push that person out. So communication is much needed, even if it is a race and nobody knows each other because they are all in it together.

Well, this is what happened to me. Somehow someone on the far left side pushed a little bit into the pack and by the time it got to me, I was kissing the concrete wall at 35 mph. I went straight over my handle bars and hit the ground like a sack of potatoes. Then all the people behind me could not help but run me over. Good thing I wore my helmet, because that got crushed under the weight of others cyclists.

It happened so fast that when all the danger was over, I looked up and saw four others like me on the ground and the rest of the pack disappearing and getting back to a normal race. Nobody looked back. I quickly got up and yelled at everyone to, "Get off the track!" because the category ones (pros) were coming up behind us. I'm sure they would freak out if they saw four people laying on the track in front of them with their bikes all spread out; besides, the pros sometimes race faster then 35 mph. So when we all got safely off to the side, we all asked if everyone was alright. We all looked at each other and then got back on our bikes after the pros went whizzing by. It was a pretty eerie feeling after the magnitude of what just happened.

There was no way we were going to be able to catch up to the pack after that, so we headed in on our broken bikes. When we got back in, I then started to notice the rips, tears and scrapes on my clothing and skin – not to mention my bike was fully trashed. I did not notice anything with my body until I got home and things were just not right. Besides a massive headache, when I went to the bathroom, my urine was blood red. Lizbeth freaked out and away we went to the hospital. They did a full C-scan on me and it turned out I punctured a big hole in my kidney from the crash. After about seven days of probably the most stress I had ever been in going to the bathroom, it slowly went away.

So how does real estate fit into all of this? It does, just on a higher level. When you get real good and are racing (taking listings daily), you will crash. When you are doing a lot of production compared to small production, there will be things that come up that you have no control over. But by knowing that they will come up makes you a smarter business person. I could have just laid there and moaned and had an ambulance come get me and play the victim, but I made a choice to get back on the bike and take responsibility for what happened. Things happen, and usually for the good. Because now I know to never, ever race next to the wall and if I find myself there, then I know what can happen. So if I want to take a risk to get to the front of the pack and know that the shortcut is the wall, then that is a choice I will have to deal with at that time.

What types of choices are you dealing with? Are you trying your hardest? Or are you on the sidelines where it is safe?

By taking up a new sport and competing in it, you will learn some of life's valuable lessons. There really is no difference in sports and business. They both take teamwork at some level and there is usually one common goal to be reached. If the sport has no team, like tennis, then you still have to get good at being a great communicator. In sports, you will have fun in the meantime and maybe even get into shape (or better shape), too.

Focus on The System For Success

You now have in your hands a perfect way to set up a great system to sell real estate and the mindset that goes with it. It is specific and you should be setting yours up now. Too many people have vague ideas of how their goals are to be. They say things like, "I want a successful team with only four people." But they never really plan it all out and see who has what job duty and why.

Through trial and error and years of experience, Lizbeth and I still make weekly changes to improve the system. It must be looked upon as *never-ending improvement*.

Live with passion daily and do not worry what others think of you. Remember, it is your life and you write the chapters of your own best seller!

The New Age Real Estate Agent

The New Age Real Estate Agent

Acknowledgements

I would like to express gratitude to my dear father who taught me the meaning of being an honest person with high integrity, for he could not have expressed it if he did not know it.
I would like to thank my mother who always put me back on the horse when I fell off and for truly believing in me no matter what.

To all my teachers that took the time to answer my questions and better yet, spent the time with me until I learned the lessons involved.

To my beautiful wife Lizbeth who has always been the wind and I the fire. To my daughter Jazmine whom I cherish every moment with, to my son Jonathan whom I love so much and to my step sons Armani and Christopher whom I care for and respect.

The New Age Real Estate Agent

Thomas and Lizbeth Hale are the successful

owners of their own;

Real Estate and Mortgage companies.

They went from a negative $60,000 in debt to a

positive net worth of more than $3 million. By

using this plan, you can do it, too! So get ready

for a life change!

The New Age Real Estate Agent